The economic ⎯⎯⎯⎯⎯⎯⎯⎯⎯⎯⎯⎯⎯⎯⎯ ⎯ions in the workplace. ⎯ ⎯⎯⎯ ⎯⎯⎯ ⎯⎯ ⎯⎯⎯ for their jobs, their financial security, and their futures. Many are also angry and confused. In *Emotional Fitness at Work*, Dr. Barton Goldsmith gives us the tools we need to keep our businesses moving forward and to help us weather this storm of panic and pain. Get it and keep it handy. The information is very useful.

—Marjory Abrams, Publisher, BottomLine Personal

Barton Goldsmith, PhD, has written a wonderful guide for business leaders and coworkers. His optimistic attitude and story telling, along with quotes from Winston Churchill to Albert Einstein, will keep you engaged throughout the book. He teaches to trust your instinct and intuition. You'll learn the importance of communication, mentoring, and balance. I highly recommend this book to anyone who is emotionally stressed, wants to improve their workplace, or is just plain curious as to how they can improve their emotional fitness.

—Bambi Holzer, author of *Set for Life* and *Financial Bliss*

Dr. Goldsmith's book tackles the most important issue facing today's executive—fear—in a straightforward, effective manner. Only by facing our fears can we overcome them; and only by overcoming our fears can we navigate the new, current realities facing our businesses. *Emotional Fitness at Work* grants us the tools we need to manage our companies to the next level. Thank you, Dr. G!

—Brad Oberwager, CEO Sundria Corp.

This book gives us all the information we need to use the power of our emotions to help us make it through this difficult and scary time. Thanks to Dr. Goldsmith, we now have a road map.

—Karen Leland, co-author of *Watercooler Wisdom: How Smart People Prosper In The Face of Conflict, Pressure and Change*

Dr. Barton Goldsmith's wise and worthy new guide, *Emotional Fitness at Work*, offers salient advice for how to navigate the workplace in a distinctly 21st-century terrain. His honest and fresh approach encourages women and men alike to contemplate how their work lives fit into their family and personal lives, and the chance to build a better model. By emphasizing trust, proactivity, compromise, and non-verbal communication, Dr. Goldsmith teaches us to use our emotions at work to our advantage.

—Susan Shapiro Barash, author of *Little White Lies, Deep Dark Secrets: The Truth about Why Women Lie*

Emotional Fitness at Work is a must-have read for anyone currently in the workforce. Using tangible examples, simple prescriptive advice, checklists and thought-provoking exercises, Dr. G gives readers hundreds of tools and ideas on how to enjoy their work, embrace their emotions in a healthy and constructive way, pave the way to take charge of their workplace experience.

—Debra Mandel, PhD, psychologist and author of *Your Boss Is Not Your Mother*

Because successful businesses are built on relationships, businesses that follow " conventional wisdom" and suppress their workers' emotions won't be successful long-term. So it's only common sense to follow Goldsmith's advice, and create a corporate culture that values emotions—one that uses specific and very worthwhile tools to harness the enormous power of positive emotions, and deal appropriately with the nuggets of necessary change delivered in the negative ones.

—Shel Horowitz, award-winning author of *Principled Profit: Marketing That Puts People First*

Emotional Fitness at Work

6 Strategic Steps to Success
Using the Power of Emotion

By Barton Goldsmith, PhD

CAREER
PRESS

Franklin Lakes, NJ

EMOTIONAL FITNESS AT WORK
EDITED BY KATE HENCHES
TYPESET BY DIANA GHAZZAWI
Cover design by Howard Grossman /12E Design
Printed in the U.S.A. by Courier

To order this title, please call toll-free 1-800-CAREER-1 (NJ and Canada: 201-848-0310) to order using VISA or MasterCard, or for further information on books from Career Press.

The Career Press, Inc., 3 Tice Road, PO Box 687,
Franklin Lakes, NJ 07417
www.careerpress.com

Library of Congress Cataloging-in-Publication Data
Goldsmith, Barton.
    Emotional fitness at work : 6 strategic steps to success using the power of emotion / by Barton Goldsmith.
        p. cm.
    Includes index.
    ISBN 978-1-60163-081-0
    1. Success in business. 2. Emotions. 3. Interpersonal relations. 4. Work--Psychological aspects. I. Title.

HF5386.G58518 2009
650.1—dc22

                                                            2009025579

It is my deep and humble honor to proudly
dedicate this book to
Peter Charles Goldsmith,
a dynamite businessman and a loving father.
Thank you for teaching me how the world really works.

Acknowledgments

Firstly, I must thank Silva, who has the gift of being able to calm me down and help me remember what is most important in life.

My literary agent, Katie Boyle, grabbed this project and had it sold in record time. Thank you for your integrity and work ethic. At Career Press, I'd like to thank acquisitions editor Michael Pye; production coordinator Jeff Piasky; editor Kirsten Dally; assistant editor Diana Ghazzawi; and editorial director Gina Talucci; for their assistance and talent.

This book wouldn't exist if not for the readers of my column, and I will be forever grateful to the editors of the hundreds of publications, who have graciously run my articles and allowed me to rant and elucidate.

The team (and my dear friends) at KCLU/NPR Radio have been nothing but supportive, innovative, and just plain fun to be around. They include Mary Olson, Jim Rondeau, Lance Orozco, Mia Karnatz-Shifflett, and Jocelyne Rohrback. Thank you also to my business partner and cohost, Dr. Stephen Trudeau, as well as the many guests who have shared their wisdom with our listening audience.

My family and friends including the Khardalians: Rafi Sr., Maggie, Christine, Anna, and Rafi Jr.; Keaton and Oliver Koechli, and David and Dan Richmond all give me a reason to be here. My team at the office, Mary Trudeau and Wendy Cherry, make my life work and remind me to eat.

I am honored to have learned from my colleagues in the (sometimes opposed) worlds of business and psychology including: Gary Chapman, Marjory Abrams, Judith Orloff, Bambi Holzer, Brad Oberwager, Joe Phelps, Mike Yeager, Susan Shapiro Barash, Kevin Hanley, Nancy Padberg, Leigh Leshner, Trygve Duryea, Jim Cathcart, Ed Rigsbee, Patti Carmalt, and George Sloan.

I have had the privilege of being a resource and working with a number of educational, leadership, and mastermind organizations. The best part is that I got to learn and grow right along with them: the Young Presidents Organization (YPO), the Young Entrepreneur's Organization (YEO), the World Presidents Organization (WPO), Vistage (formally TEC—The Executive Committee), and the Council of Growing Companies.

I have also had the opportunity to speak to many businesses and associations around the world and those experiences have helped to shape the ideas shared in this book. The list is too long to mention, but thank you all, and I am honored that you continue to allow me to share my experiences, ideas, and a few jokes.

Lastly, I wish to thank those people and companies who have hired me as a business and executive consultant and given the greatest gift of all: their trust.

Contents

Preface

For more than a decade, I have written business columns that have run in more than 500 publications. I have consulted for many companies at all levels of business and given numerous speeches on the psychology of work. My focus has been on harnessing the emotions of team members and companies and using these emotions to grow a successful business. After the economic crisis began, I received many more e-mails requesting copies of articles pertaining to the role of emotions in the workplace, and requests for more information and a place where readers could go to "get it all." So I have created and compiled the best information available in hopes that it will help deal with the stresses we are all currently facing.

Just for the record, I do not come to this from the perspective of a "shrink" but rather that of a successful businessman. I only returned to school as something to do between projects after I sold my third company. I never intended to practice but rather planned to use the knowledge I gained to consult for business.

This book is for more than just the business professional. That is, you don't have to be a boss or a manager to be a good leader; developing those traits can help you, no matter what your job description. That being said, if you don't want to get better at what you do, or don't at least have the desire to understand more about business, you wouldn't have picked up this book.

Introduction

"There's no crying in baseball!": the truth about emotions in business

In the film *A League of Their Own*, Tom Hanks chastises one of his players, and she begins to cry. "Are you crying?" asks Hanks. "There's no crying. There's no crying in baseball!" Yet, baseball and business are emotional games, and feelings are everywhere. The emotions created by a World Series or an economic meltdown are tremendous. How does what is happening with the stock market, foreclosures, bailouts, and failures make you feel? Enormous amounts of emotions abound from Wall Street to Main Street. The loss of wealth and financial security has created an outpouring of fear, pain, and anger from almost everyone in America. But we do have some power here because a business can also generate as much emotion in its people as a first-place team can generate in its teammates and fans.

In reality, however, most business professionals try to keep emotions out of business. After all, emotions running rampant make things difficult. Why? Emotional team members can have a significant negative impact on performance. Emotional people can perform erratically, engage in arguments, and refuse to work together. The results are generally a clash of egos and the loss of productivity.

Understanding feelings at work

One of the ways negative emotions present themselves in the workplace is in team members withdrawing and being unavailable to their coworkers. This is a reaction to fear or hurt feelings. To put it in Psych 101 terms: People act out their pain. In the workplace, they tend to respond emotionally because the people with whom they work on a daily basis become a surrogate family, and people tend to react and respond like family members. If the family/company has good communication skills and thrives on interaction, people act in a functional manner, and resolve differences appropriately. If, however, the family/company is dysfunctional, or is reeling from external influences (like the financial downturn), it brings up emotions. When this happens, team members (who are only human) often act very much like children playing in a sandbox—"Your truck ran over my truck," and "I'm not playing with you anymore."

Furthermore, when people get their feelings hurt, they can become unconscious saboteurs. This can manifest in a number of ways including not contributing at meetings, missing deadlines, and even offending clients. Ninety-nine percent of the time, this is unconscious behavior. People are not aware they are doing it because the unconscious controls 90 percent of our actions. If unhealed emotions are not addressed, companies can experience significant losses in terms of personnel, a dwindling customer base, financial success, and market positioning.

The keys to motivation

All businesses want motivated team members. They spend time and money pumping up and motivating staff. They want to build passion, and what is passion but emotion? So on the one hand, companies work to create feelings (when it serves them) and on the other they attempt to suppress them when they suit their immediate needs. Truth is, you can't have one without the other. But you can balance emotions and maintain an emotionally healthy business environment.

Emotional and passionate people make things happen, but they are not encouraged in business settings where detached, cool, and objective decision-making skills are considered to be strengths. Passionate people threaten the status quo. They create change and shake things up. Their passion begets persistence. Motivation, creativity, and productivity are the energy boosters businesses want, but what is your company doing to create that culture?

Meeting the challenge

Today's executives spend half their time being a therapist to their staff, solving their (mostly interpersonal) problems. It is difficult to conceive the amount of time and energy that are lost. Once team members learn to understand and deal with emotions, that time could be put to building the company. Some companies have staff therapists or executive coaches, some do emotional release sessions, and others use team-building exercises. All of these efforts add directly to the bottom line. Your challenge is to create a culture that understands the losses suffered from negative emotions and utilize the power of positive emotions. That is exactly what *Emotional Fitness at Work* is going to give you.

Taking the first step

How you use this book will depend in part on if you are an employee, manager, or executive running a business. Some of the chapters may be as much for teammates who are trying to get along better with others and communicate more effectively with their bosses as they are for the CEO.

It is not important that you read the book from beginning to end. Skipping around is just as valid as a start-to-finish approach. If you are dealing with a particular issue, you can go straight to that part of the book that covers it. For example, you may be more interested in Understanding Emotions and Success (page 19) than you are in Resolving Conflicts (page 61), or vice versa.

All six steps are applicable to most everyone in the workplace, but you can't eat the whole pie at once, so go with what works best for you. I believe that if we are Working Well With Others (page 103), we will be much more likely to achieve success, and under the current economic circumstances, Crisis Management (page 127) and Mentoring and Motivating (page 157) are two very important steps that cannot be overlooked.

For those who are running a company, improving your Leadership Skills (page 197) should always be on your radar screen. Learning to be an emotionally centered leader will give your company a leg up on the competition. We are all looking to keep afloat and prosper. By utilizing the power of emotions we can survive the crisis and move forward. Your business life will be much easier, more successful, and a whole lot more enjoyable.

Understanding Emotions and Success

Emotions are a constant in the business universe, and to navigate successfully, you need to understand and harness their energy. From the success principles of the best in business to dealing with economic fears, this step educates the reader on the role emotions play for both the individual and his or her team. Whether we engage in self-sabotage or are unable to achieve our goals, there are tools available to help us utilize the power of emotion to pursue new ideas. It's not just about thinking outside the box; it's about getting comfortable with the feelings those thoughts create. There is no perfection, but you can have a lot of fun and make money when you learn to deal with the best business tool you have: your emotional strength.

Dr. G's Top 10 Success Principles

It takes 20 years to make an overnight success.
—Eddie Cantor

Becoming successful is an art form; staying successful takes a lot of work. Here are 10 tools that I've seen the "best of the best" use to achieve and maintain success. Using them will help you and your team.

1. You have what it took to get you here. But becoming a success is easier than staying successful. Focus on the great things that you do and remember that greatness in one area spills over into other areas. Believing in yourself is an incredibly potent force that will take you and your team to the next level.

2. Trust your gut. Relying on your instincts is what the Warren Buffetts and Jack Welches do on a daily basis. Sure, you might not be right every time, but each success makes your skill set stronger. Try keeping track of your "hunches" for a couple of weeks and follow the results.

3. You're either green and growing, or ripe and rotting. Continue to educate yourself and learn as much as you can about what you are currently doing and what you want to do in the future. Be sure that the people around you do the same.

4. Live life on your own terms. If you're doing what feels right, trust it. If you want something more or different, declare it for yourself and create an achievable plan to get there. You get to decide what success means to you and no one else. The ultimate success is having the ability to call your own shots.

5. Realize that women and men measure their worth differently. Think about how you would view yourself if you were the opposite gender. Stop trying to "have it all," because somewhere along the line you will accidentally drop something very important. In addition, the stress can kill you or at least make your work and/or life a living hell.

6. Remember that money isn't the root of all evil; people (rich or poor) are. Wealth only corrupts the corruptible. Money makes you more of what you already are. If you don't like what you've become, remember that you have the power to change. By the way, negative thoughts about money can stop you from making it. Be open to becoming one of the people and companies that flourish in the downturn.

7. Know when to stop telling and start asking. The best leaders ask a lot of clarifying questions and offer brilliant solutions. There's power in knowing how to ask the right questions, and there's a lot more power when your clients and coworkers know you care.

8. Trust your inner (hyperactive) child. Most leaders know how to do several things at the same time and be very effective. Delegation, concentration, and imagination will all serve you well. Focus on the task at hand, but, when a team member requires your attention, be 100-percent there. Yes, you can think of and do more than one thing at a time. You wouldn't be successful if you didn't multitask.

9. Value people more than money. The heart weighs more than the wallet. It's about being able to help people with your

success, not about how many toys you can buy. You can't put a price on feeling good about yourself and how you have had a positive impact on the world and those you care for.

10. Never stop reading. Make the effort to read material that is outside your normal field of interest. Integrating what you know with new information is where great ideas come from. Always carry a book or have some new reading material on your BlackBerry, you never know when you'll get stuck waiting and this way you won't waste a second.

The people I know who are truly successful are some of the most gracious and generous individuals on the planet. When people are truly feeling as if they are sharing their talents with the world, it gives them a good reason to help others by mentoring them and helping improve their lives. Set a good example for how living successfully can make you, your company, and the world a better place to be.

Coping With Economic Fears

We have nothing to fear but fear itself.
—Franklin D. Roosevelt

Since the financial crisis began, Americans have been experiencing a new dynamic in their everyday lives; some are only feeling a slight pinch (for now), while others are living with the fear of complete financial devastation. This feeling is present in every area of our lives, and creates new challenges for business leaders and professionals of all levels.

Beyond the current losses in real estate and on Wall Street, we have lost something much more valuable. Our peace of mind has been irrevocably altered, and we will never be the same again. The upshot for business is that our risk tolerance has been significantly lowered, and this affects everyone in a company from the CEO on down.

This feeling takes some getting used to (not that we want to do that). Living with fear changes the way people behave in every aspect of their lives. It affects our ability to "be professional" and makes us reorient our priorities. Frankly, it's irritating being in fear. It's like being in a lawsuit: it can suck the life out of you.

Fear affects our productivity, our communications, our ability to create, and our emotional well being. In order for us to deal with this new threat, we must first and foremost learn to identify its existence. Without the ability to identify the problem, it will only get worse and weaken the structure of our lives and businesses. Living in denial will only hold us back, and it will create a country that stops functioning because everyone is angry and scared.

In order to decide what to do about it, people have to be encouraged to talk. Our lives are being permeated by words such as "meltdown," "depression," "recession," and "bailout." People are afraid to spend money, or even leave it in the bank, and businesses are closing daily.

The business community is in a position to do a great deal to alleviate fear. The first step is to make it safe for your people to talk about what they are feeling.

This may sound "touchy-feely," but there is a real bottom line payoff to understanding how this is affecting your business, as well as your life. With the highest unemployment in decades, people are in fear of their livelihood and, in some cases, just basic survival. If you can't see how that would affect your business, then you'd better take some time and think about it. The decisions you make now will affect your company, your life, and the lives of the people that work with you.

Anyone who has run a company for several years has seen a few downturns. In some small and closely held businesses, staff are kept on even during difficult times because people in them relate as much like a family as they do a business. In the majority of private and almost all public companies, decisions about layoffs are based on the bottom line and staff members know it. If you don't get them talking, they will act out their feelings of fear and could unconsciously make or avoid decisions that affect the entire company.

Getting the process started may be the biggest challenge. It's the old "400-pound gorilla under the table" syndrome; we all know it's there and we can't escape it, but we can't bring ourselves to talk about how it really makes us feel. Taking that step requires some finesse, and it may not be something anyone in your company feels comfortable doing.

This may be an instance where bringing in a professional counselor is a company's best choice. Most HR professionals (although very capable at their jobs) may not have the skill set to deal with this kind of intensity. Bringing in a professional also allows everyone in the company to participate in dealing with the issue by freeing up the CEO and HR department to partake in the process, rather than facilitate it. In addition, your company's health insurance may cover the cost, but if not, considering the value, it's a lot cheaper than bankruptcy.

But first things first, get your team talking and do some talking yourself. Verbalizing feelings really works. There is no question about it, so stop wondering and start the dialogue. Think of it as an investment that has an immediate payoff.

Do You Sabotage Your Success?

*Success is often the result of taking a misstep
in the right direction.*
—Al Bernstein

Even when the economy as a whole is purring along, negative emotions play a role in your business life. Those feelings are one of the many ways to sabotage your own success. For example, some people, who say they want success, are terrified of the responsibility that goes along with being a success. They think, "If I am successful with this business, I'll have to be responsible for taxes, insurance, employees and their livelihoods." That thought can become overwhelming, and some will choose not to experience the success because they have an inhibiting fear; or, individuals can engage in self-sabotage by berating themselves, perhaps, because they feel they are a fraud of some sort, and surely someone is bound to pull the covers and expose them for being just another member of the human race. These are just a few obstacles that get in the way of success and need to be addressed.

Understanding what stops us

One of the best ways to overcome self-sabotage is to identify the source of the problem. There was a CEO who received an invitation to be a guest speaker for a very prestigious organization. Instead of being thrilled, he thought the meeting planner sent the invitation to the wrong person. This reaction, which is indicative of limiting doubts and fears regarding success, usually has its roots in the past. The belief was that the CEO did not think he had what it took to earn the right to speak before this group. But the FACT is that he was already successful and on the way to becoming even more successful. He was standing on the precipice of doing the work he had wanted to do all of his life, and it was scary.

The rationalization syndrome

When fear erupts, people create safety nets to catch themselves if they fall. In this case the CEO above created the false belief that he didn't deserve the success yet, so that if it didn't come, he could rationalize his disappointment. Now ask yourself: have I ever killed the deal in my head, by thinking I was out of my league, before the meeting began? At that point, you disempowered yourself.

Those false beliefs are part of a syndrome. They keep you very safe; they also keep you from achieving your goals. You don't have to change and no one around you has to change. Everyone and everything stays right where they are, safe inside the "box." There's a lot of mileage to be found in beliefs that keep you from being all you can. Ask yourself: where are you in your life that you believe you aren't worthy and what kind of mileage are you getting out of it?

Everything changes

Success is a change, and even though it is a positive one, it can cause many uncomfortable feelings. Success changes circumstances, and it changes people. Keep in mind you cannot control the reactions of others. Some people may not know how to approach you. Others, especially those you have known for some time, may be envious. You may even begin to feel guilty about your success.These are somewhat normal reactions and need to be addressed as such.Talk with the people to whom you are closest, let them encourage you, and don't forget to encourage yourself.

The cure

Acknowledging success brings more of it to you.Not accepting success is a way to avoid it. One of the ways people can be unaccepting is to gloss over their successes.They don't take the time to acknowledge and reward their own accomplishments.This is easily healed, but seldom done. Simply spend some time congratulating yourself and celebrate your success.Take yourself out to dinner or buy yourself something.Small and frequent celebrations create inspiration. If you are inspired, you will create more success and better serve your family, company, and clients.

You have the answers

Think about things you can do to continue moving forward in this thinking.Begin to examine what scares you in life,what beliefs keep you from accepting success.With a little effort, you will see things differently,and never again sabotage success.After all,your success didn't fall from the sky, you earned it.

Look for the Pony

4

You don't pay the price for success.
You enjoy the price for success.
—Zig Ziglar

If you've had a failure at work, know that you are now better prepared to take on the next project. If you're frightened for your survival because your company is reeling from the financial roller-coaster ride we are all on, that's normal. To combat this negative emotional fallout, it is important to take an optimistic approach and start letting your team know that you believe that your next year will be a better one than most others will have, and take the appropriate steps to make that happen.

Many of my readers have commented on my optimistic outlook on business and life. When anyone asks how I developed this attitude, I share a story (attributed to Ronald Reagan) about a "study" done at a university.

Two preteen boys, one pessimistic and the other optimistic, were put in different rooms. The pessimistic kid was in a room with the latest toys and gadgets, and the optimistic one was put in a room with a huge pile of horse manure.

When the researchers returned an hour later, they found the pessimistic boy in a corner. He had pushed all the toys and gadgets to the side and was whimpering that he was afraid he would break something and get into trouble. When they entered the room with the optimistic boy, they found him enthusiastically digging in the pile. When they asked him why he was so excited, he exclaimed, "With all this, there must be a pony in here somewhere!"

All the clichés you've ever heard (every cloud has a silver lining; when one door closes, another opens; and so on) have been created and maintained by people who have lived them. The hard part is believing that things will get brighter when all you can see is the darkness.

Your perspective about this may have to grow through time. If you have never experienced a business loss that has been followed by a success, then it's hard to perceive that it could happen to you. The truth is that, for most people who are willing to make the effort and take a little risk, most obstacles can be overcome. Luckily, the next phase is often much better than the one that ended.

The trick is to not allow yourself to wallow in self-pity or be paralyzed by fear, and, instead, put yourself out there and go after what you want. I promise that, if you sit around waiting for good things to come to you, the only thing you will receive is disappointment.

It may be hard to see when life is standing on your neck, but there are millions of successful people who will tell you that they got where they are by pushing themselves beyond their comfort levels. It's true that you run the risk of someone saying no or getting disappointed yet again, but that's the point. You have to take a shot if you want to change your life for the better.

One of the most powerful positions you can take in life is to know that, if you were to lose everything, you could find success once again. I pray that you never have to go through anything so difficult, but if you do, you can trust that you have the inner strength and confidence to make your world whole again.

The Lost Art of Goal Achievement

People are not lazy. They simply have impotent goals—
that is, goals that do not inspire them.
—Anthony Robbins

After consulting for more than 300 companies and doing presentations for a couple thousand more, I have found that they all have one thing in common: Businesses all over the world have had to face the fact that goal-setting is a lot easier than goal-achieving.

I have seen dozens of impressively bound and documented strategic plans collecting dust after the goals set at the expensive off-site were unrealized. There are any number of excuses that prevented success: fires that had to be put out, the economy, or my dog ate my homework. As a seasoned strategic planner, I have the right to say, "I hate it when that happens."

The reason most goals don't reach fruition is that the people who created them did it to please someone else—say, their CEO. Instead, your team needs to be set free to put into motion ideas that they feel strongly about and that will be beneficial to the company and its team members. Emotions are the key.

35

When people have their emotions attached to a goal, it is achieved. If you think this is too simple, you're right. The problem in business today is that we forget the power of having real buy-in versus agreeing to what the top dogs think they want. Team members will always give into the ideas of those who hold the power of the paycheck because everyone thinks about their survival first.

So, here is a plan to get you team to not just set goals, but achieve big, fat, hairy ones. First, let's reconsider the idea of SMART goals (Specific, Measurable, Achievable, Realistic, Timely). This acronym has done more damage to business motivation than Dilbert.

The real truth is that, if team members have their hearts in it, they will get to the finish line. I know the mere mention of hearts will make the "tough guys" cringe, but I've been doing this long enough to know that creating emotional buy-in works. The problem is that some leaders work long and hard to avoid "feelings" in the workplace. Today's managers and leaders need to learn to use emotions to their advantage instead of being scared of them.

The first step in harnessing this untapped resource is to believe in it. If that's a problem for you, just look at how you got to where you are in your life. Would you be here if you didn't have your heart in it? Now, how do you create that same drive, buy-in, commitment, and power in your team? Well, as Obi-Wan guided Luke Skywalker, "Trust your feelings."

Use your gift of intuition (and I don't know one successful leader who doesn't have it) to guide you in asking your people what it is about the direction of your company that's important to them. Once you have an alignment and you give them the power to create their vision, then all you have to do is to get out of their way. This final step can be harder for some than for others.

Empower your team members by really supporting them in reaching the goals that they believe are best for the company. It will not only help you reach beyond your nicely packaged strategic plan; it will boost your profits to a level that only those who use this hidden force have been able to enjoy.

The Enriching Power of Self-Evaluations

There are three things extremely hard: steel, a diamond, and to know one's self.
—Benjamin Franklin

I firmly believe that if you want to grow personally and/or professionally you have to take an honest look at where you are, before you can decide where you want to (or are able to) go—and where you want to take others. Doing a serious self-evaluation at least once a year is necessary to keep up your current pace, and, if you want your business to grow at an accelerated rate, I suggest doing it twice a year.

I have created 10 self-evaluation questions for you that will help you create a positive dialogue and make the process more effective then a typical performance or 360 review. These questions will be great fuel for helping you understand how progress is being made and what course corrections are necessary. It also opens the door for some serious career mentoring. Most importantly, it will help you discover the skills that need to be developed in order to achieve your goals.

These questions are not designed for quick answers. This is not a race. Take your time and feel as well as think about how you can most honestly answer these questions. Read the entire list before you begin your process, and allow each question to digest slowly. Taking your time with this evaluation will give you the best insights.

Self-Evaluation Questions for Business

1. What are my business goals for the next year?
2. What changes do I need to make in my professional relationships?
3. What are the biggest business difficulties for the next year?
4. Do I need to reconsider doing business with a client/customer this year?
5. Who am I not working well with, and how can I make it better?
6. What business issues keep me up at night?
7. What have I learned about myself while working at this job?
8. Am I doing all I can to keep the company on track?
9. Do I enjoy my job most of the time? If not, what can I do to make it better?
10. What can I do to make the people with whom I work as comfortable as possible?

If you need to make changes in either your business or personal life, first write down exactly what it is you want to change. Having written goals gives you a 300-percent better chance of reaching them. Next, find someone to share the goals with and to help hold you accountable. Your mentor is the ideal choice, and if you don't have one, or are not a member of a mastermind group, add "find a mentor" to your list (and read Chapter 50 on mastermind groups).

Lastly, and most importantly, review your goals daily. I advise posting them near your computer (even on your screen saver) or on your desk so you see them often. This will serve as a subconscious reinforcement and will aid you in reaching your goals in less time. Making one significant change per month is appropriate for most people. Remember: If you try to eat the whole pie at once, you'll make yourself sick.

These self-evaluations are perhaps the most powerful tool you can use to boost your productivity at work and the enjoyment of both your life and career. If deeper questions or concerns arise, talk with someone you trust and be proactive by taking the steps necessary to create balance where it is needed. It's your life. No one is going to make it better but you.

"Shrink" Like a Leader

There are no office hours for leaders.
—Cardinal J. Gibbons

Business leaders have used a multitude of tactics and techniques to motivate, activate, stimulate, encourage, revitalize, and inspire their teams. And some of these tools are very useful (see my suggestions in Chapters 6 through 8). Unfortunately much of what is still used in today's workplace is yesterday's technology. Take, for example, the Myers-Briggs and DISC personality type indicators. They are both several generations old! In addition, most managers don't have the psychological training necessary to utilize the information gained from these assessment tools. Leaders require more up-to-date information that can actually be put to use.

If you really look at how your business uses the "oldies," you will see that most team members kinda shrug off the information about their personalities. What they really need and want are recognition and a pleasant working environment, so they can enjoy what they're doing. The number-one reason people leave their jobs is because they don't get along with their bosses. Though these tests do give some information into the underlying psychological nuances of team members, they are really more of a curiosity than a team-building tool for today's businesses.

There are more current personality indicators that can be accessed on the Web at no cost. But the question remains: is it personality or personal responsibility that makes a great team member or leader? Most psychological indicators can tell you how you think, but can they tell you how to think like a leader?

There is an upside to not thinking like a leader. If everyone did, you'd have no one working for you. Instead they'd be competition. In order to get the most out of team members and also be able to keep them, here are a couple of facts that will help you. First, remember that recognition is the number-one motivator of human beings. The handshake in front of other people (especially management) and the handwritten thank-you note are just of couple of the ways you can boost your team morale and your bottom line.

Next, if you manage like Attila the Hun, your team members will never go the extra mile. They will dread coming into work and they won't be inspired to think about how to make your business or department excel. Instead they will be filling out applications online and spend the time you are paying them for trying to get on a reality TV show.

Being nice may sound namby-pamby, but the real truth is that every time you put out a little positive energy it comes back to you. Sadly, I have seen very successful companies go under because the CEO was unwilling to simply compliment his or her staff members.

Take a lesson from those who have failed; learn from their mistakes and learn how to motivate your team with solid psychology. My essays are used by a number of colleges and universities in their management classes and, whenever I am asked to comment, I always say that today's top leaders need to have the skill set equivalent to a master's degree in business and a doctorate in psychology.

Pursuing Failure

Success is going from failure to failure
without loss of enthusiasm.
—Winston Churchill

Most people dislike the idea of failure, but, if you really think about it, the only way not to fail is by not trying. Wouldn't you rather your people try, at the risk of failing, to attempt new ideas, seek to bring in new clients, and try to create new products, than not? If your people are not allowed to fail, they will not grow. If you cannot encourage your team to reach new heights by giving them a safety net (not firing them if they fail), then how will you take your company to the next level?

From 0 to 50...million

This philosophy has helped a number of companies reach the top of their markets. Take, for example, Mid-America Direct. CEO Mike Yager continues to encourage his team to try new ideas, and he doesn't punish them if the ideas don't work right away. He believes that with support, his team members will reach deep within

43

themselves and create new income streams for the company. He continues to remind them that they are part of a team and that they are supported, by him and by each other. Even if their ideas don't work, he is pleased that they are attempting to push the envelope. To further inspire his people, they also get personal rewards for continued efforts in improving the company.

Yager started his company with a vision, ideas like this, and not much else. He believes that the only thing that can turn a challenge into a failure is not learning from it. He also believes in continuing education for his team and brings in the best speakers and trainers in the country to help his people reach the next level.

Act as if

Being able to look at your failures and learn from them is a definition of wisdom. To be able to see them clearly, as steps to your goals, gives you energy and inspiration. If you beat yourself up, and become listless with self-loathing, your goals become harder to reach. The energy you put into anger just holds you, and your people, back. If you have difficulty grasping this idea, here's a way to see how it actually works.

The next time you or one of your team members fails, don't chastise him (or yourself). Hold back your anger or disappointment and "act as if" (pretend) it was part of the process. See it as a step in the right direction. Talk with your team, and explain that you believe that this supposed "failure" is taking you closer to your goal. Explain to them (and yourself) that without the lessons learned from this failure, you would not have the information and experience necessary to achieve success. Then see if you don't reach the next level quicker and easier than if you spent time and energy wallowing in blame, anger, and disappointment. This isn't some kind of mind game; it's a necessary step in growing your business that has been used by some of the most successful leaders and companies in the world.

Beyond failure

Perhaps the most important job of a leader is to help his or her people learn from their mistakes. This is the learning that comes from experience, and it's the most valuable learning we can experience. By supporting your team and yourself in this kind of thinking, you are creating a company culture that will inspire your team to make your business grow. Most successful people will honestly tell you that they reached their goals by making lots of mistakes. The leader's job is to encourage people to reach beyond their failures, mistakes and fears, and use the lessons learned to achieve success. Work to encourage your team to pursue failure, and they will respond by pushing the envelope all the way to the top, helping your company survive the current economic downturn and thrive in the near future.

Outside-the-Box Business

Creative minds have always been known to
survive any kind of bad training.
—Anna Freud

Today, thinking "outside the box" is not enough. Companies have to live outside the box in order to create meaningful business change. For example, instead of holding a strategic planning meeting at the home office or in a local hotel, take the entire team to an inspirational and unusual location—Bora-Bora, for example. Why? Because your team will think much differently in Bora-Bora than they will in the same familiar surroundings. I understand that in the current economic climate a trip like that is akin to the CEOs of the Big 3 auto-makers coming to D.C. with their hands out in private jets, so it might be best to find a suitable location closer to home. The main point here is that when one's entire being is immersed in a different environment, the people there can't help but think more creatively and with greater passion.

If planning meetings are continually held in the office, participants will likely provide the same thoughts and ideas they have always offered. Companies that are not satisfied with the business-as-usual approach seek innovation and creativity from their people first by setting the scene. They hold important meetings, such as strategic-planning, team-building, and problem-solving meetings in a destination and manner that inspire the participants. The result is a shift in perspective, which often produces solutions that were previously not considered. That's part of outside-the-box business.

Inventiveness and change are the byproducts of seeing things differently. When this happens, possibilities begin to flow. Suddenly new ideas of what companies (or people) want and how to get there reveal themselves. A shift in business perspective can open many doors. Once the door is open, the hard work has been done. Then the risk of stepping through it doesn't seem quite as scary.

The facilitator

To maximize contributions and creativity, it's important for the CEO or top management executives to participate in, but not dominate, the meeting. Why? If the CEO is the facilitator, participants tend to echo the leader's ideas, and the CEO may unconsciously push his or her own desires. That format doesn't encourage outside-the-box thinking. In addition, facilitation is a skill that most leaders don't possess. The facilitator needs to be able to push the meeting forward and free up the CEO to add creativity, not leadership.

What's the alternative? Hire a pro to run your meeting or bring in someone from another department. Trained facilitators help people open their minds to new ideas and new methods that may feel uneasy at first, but are necessary to birth change. In other words, they help meeting participants see things differently and create new and better ideas and goals.

Overcoming limitations

The "box" is really a comfort zone. It is where people feel at ease, where they feel safe. There is nothing wrong with feeling comfortable and safe. However, if you look at the accomplishments of great thinkers, business leaders, performers, athletes, and artists, you will see they reach the pinnacle of success in their respective fields because they choose to move beyond what was comfortable, what is known. They begin to *think* differently, which leads them to see things differently and, in turn, to *do* things differently. They all have taken risks and stepped out of their comfort zone in order to achieve their goals.

For example, Edison rarely slept. Instead he took naps, with a rock in his hand! He did this because when he fell from the dream state, where he got his ideas, into deep sleep, the rock would fall and wake him up. He was then able to remember his dreams, and that is how he got the ideas for his many inventions.

Innovation requires high-risk challenges to business. Successful leaders and entrepreneurs take risks, and step out of their comfort zones. Whatever the greatest fear, they face it and find ways to walk through it. Consulting with a mentor or a high-level executive coach can help jump that hurdle. Most importantly, remember that, though there is risk in trying something new, no matter what the outcome, there is no failure. And don't expect to do it all or right the first time. Even for the most successful, risk-taking and tolerance are learned skills. Great leaders don't prepare to fail. They do, however, accept not achieving all their dreams at once, and they never give up.

When people are the first to do something new in life, whether it's a first job, or creating a new product, it usually takes a long time. That also applies to any new venture, whether it is opening a business, selling a company, or retiring. New territory is definitely outside the comfort zone even if it's a lifelong dream. Once navigated, the terrain of a new process becomes familiar, and doing it again will become much easier.

Repetition can ease the anxiety of a difficult task. For example, after growing and selling a first business, there is much less anxiety starting and growing the second. The same principle holds true when beginning to think differently. Most successful executives find that, whatever challenge they accept, they may feel awful and awkward the first time. Yet, the second time they do it, they have more command of the situation. There's no question that it is uncomfortable venturing into unknown waters. Yet, it is crucial in order to reach new levels in one's professional and personal life. Remember: The only people who are wrong are those who say, "It can't be done."

The idea zone

In today's marketplace, a willingness to stretch and to grow is essential. The world is changing rapidly, and a new approach to business and management is necessary to meet the demands of these shifting times. Accept the challenge. Go beyond the fray. Step out of your comfort zone, and see the limitless possibilities that exist.

By conquering the very things that terrify people the most, the boundaries literally melt away. Obstacles that have held people back all their lives become stepping-stones to a new vision. As people develop new, shared visions, others will follow because of the convictions proponents have. That's when people experience the exhilaration, freedom, and power of the zone outside-the-box business. They are living in the "idea zone." This is where joy, success, creativity, and personal power reside.

The Persian Flaw

Certain flaws are necessary for the whole.
—Johann Goethe

There is a legend that ancient rug makers wove an intentional flaw into their carpets. The reason was to remind us of our humanness and that only a higher power could make something perfect. If only we could remember that basic truth when we get upset at our teammates.

I often wonder why people are so hard on each other when a mistake is made. Ask yourself how many times you have lost it when a coworker made an error—perhaps similar to one that you have made in the past. It would seem only natural to give him or her some understanding that he or she is mortal and mistakes do happen.

If there is premeditated maliciousness at hand, that's a different story. Intentional wrongdoing is never appropriate and sometimes not forgivable. We all need to maintain boundaries to keep ourselves and our companies safe. Having boundaries also keeps us from going overboard when we get tweaked at someone we work with (or for). Remember that getting even with someone actually leaves you with less.

It's not that mistakes shouldn't be acknowledged. When you see someone doing something that could result in a financial or client loss (or even a stain on the carpet), you need to let him or her know it. But how you do this makes a difference. Be straightforward and kind. Communicating through sarcasm can leave an emotional wound, and the only thing you may learn is to avoid the person who gave it to you.

Fortunately, those who are forgiving by nature will find a way to overlook or understand the minor flaws of teammates. The rest of us may need to learn the technique through trial and error or, better yet, through the example of those who have overlooked our own mistakes.

Being able to admit when you are wrong is also a good trait. It can bring you new clients and help you keep the business you've got.

This ability can be especially valuable in working relationships. When someone has to be perfect all the time, it can make communication difficult, if not impossible. It can also create a great deal of discomfort and inhibition, because you're afraid of being chastised by someone with whom you work. If your teammates or boss is looking for flaws, trust me, he or she is going to find them. The trick here is to give everyone a little room to be human.

Accepting the fact that we are all going to slip and slide through this ride called life is a great tool. It will make you easier on those around you and yourself. Perfection is only possible in the movies.

Living and doing business in the real world is never going to be a fantasy. What we need to understand is that reality is the only vehicle we have to make our dreams come true.

So trust that, even if your business isn't a magic carpet ride at the moment, in the end, it's still a beautiful work of art.

Remember to Have Fun

*People rarely succeed unless they have fun
in what they are doing.*
—Dale Carnegie

In companies where people have fun, the productivity and the profit are higher. The American Psychological Association has published surveys about this, and it's a fact. Take the example of Southwest Airlines: "A sense of humor" is on their job application! I believe that this attitude and culture has helped their business become one of the major success stories of our time. During the spike in fule costs, when all the airlines were having major downturns, Southwest was still in the black. I believe this was because their sense of humor attitude made people feel comfortable to fly with them, and they didn't have to raise fares.

Attitude

Attitude and behavior are a choice, and I believe in banning bad attitudes. A great technique to integrate this culture into your business is to begin with a simple strategy called "Good Attitude

Wednesday." Every Wednesday, everyone is in a good mood—no bad attitudes allowed. This energy is infectious; you can't be in a bad mood when everyone around you is in a good mood. Once you begin, it's easy to extend this into the rest of the week. The effect will appear in your bottom line, and lower turnover will be one of the many side benefits.

Eliminate negativity from the workplace

If you've ever had to let someone go because of a negative attitude, you probably got a response from the rest of the team that was something like, "What took you so long?" One negative person can bring down an entire workforce. When that person walks into the front door, the feeling he brings with him is almost palpable; you can feel it. It's like a fog that causes dampened spirits in everyone. In one company, where I consulted, they had an individual who, though he was very important to the company and doing a highly detailed task, was a misanthrope. This person did not like people, and people did not like him. Through some quality brainstorming, we came up with an idea that was a little off-beat, but seemed to serve everyone well. The CEO decided to clean out a storage closet, and put in a desk and computer so that this individual could have his own office. He would come in to the office in the morning carrying his lunch, go into his office, close the door behind him, and leave at the end of the day. He was happy because he had an office of his own, and the staff was happy because they no longer had to contend with his negativity. Whether you have to let someone go, or find him or her a place where he or she won't interfere with the rest of your team, I urge you to do it sooner rather than later.

Implement fun experiences

Keeping the energy high and incorporating fun takes a little thought, but there are many simple and inexpensive ways to do this. Every now and then, bring in something different and uplifting for your team, like an ice cream cart, a popcorn machine, or a cappuccino maker (you may actually want to keep this one). Bowling parties, outdoor meetings, off-the-wall celebrations, and awards are other ways to uplift people and get them thinking outside the box. It also builds that esprit de corps, or the team spirit, that seems to fade away during difficult economic times, such as we are currently facing. It doesn't take much thought and usually doesn't cost much money to help people have a good time. Even something as simple as "Hawaiian Shirt Day" can turn a slow quarter into a positive attitude for the next quarter.

10 Tools for Emotional Communications

Communication is a skill that you can learn.
—Brian Tracy

All communication, the most important thing in any business, is emotionally based. Upon occasion it can be neutral, like in a text or an e-mail, but in most cases the sender will project some type of feeling that has the power to inspire or offend the receiver. Leaders or team members who can get their messages across clearly and concisely will not only maintain the respect of their coworkers; they will also reap the benefits of a healthy work environment and strong bottom line. Learn these techniques and, more importantly, use them. Your work life will be more productive and positive.

    1. Balance speaking and listening. We have all experienced certain people who like to speak just so they can hear themselves talk. The good leader will control not only his or her input but also the contributions of the staff in attendance. The good team member will wait for the right moment to give appropriate suggestions or comments and then openly listen to the feedback.

2.   Communication is a learned skill. If you don't see yourself as a top-flight communicator, get some coaching; it's not hard to learn the tricks of the trade, and the positive results will astound you. One of the best tools out there is Toastmasters (*www.toastmasters.org*). Joining and participating in this group will help you refine all of your communications, public and private.

3.   Learn and use communication styles that work in the workplace. If you know a person's style you can easily read between the lines and really understand what it is he or she is trying to say (or trying to cover up). Discovering your own communication style will help you to enhance your interactions with team members and let you get your point across in the most effective manner possible.

4.   Read nonverbal messages. Understanding that people don't always mean what they say is an essential component in fostering high-end communication. If you get good at reading nonverbal messages and watching how team members treat (and talk about) each other, you will gain a deeper understanding of what is going on in your company.

5.   Listen for the emotion behind what's being communicated. Therapists call this listening with the third ear. Knowing how a person honestly feels will help you to see his or her motivation and what it is he or she really wants and/or needs. Without this knowledge, it can be problematic for you to keep your company on track.

6.   Anonymous forms don't work. Insisting that team members take surveys and openly discuss or write about issues with others on your staff, or the company doesn't work. What you want to set up is the opportunity for them to state their feelings in an arena where there will be no reprisals and where they don't feel as though they are being disloyal to a fellow team member. In addition, most people know that, even if a management survey is supposed to be confidential, the higher-ups can figure out who said what, so you won't get the whole truth using that technique.

7. Prepare for the inevitable communication crisis. When communication breaks down, it's stressful and takes your team away from the business of doing business. Start by creating a game plan with different modalities for people and departments. Create a communications team and give them some training so they can help diffuse the inevitable crisis.

8. Repair problems in a timely manner. Letting people linger while you're making a decision that can affect their jobs costs your company money and messes with their sense of well-being, and they won't be able to do their best work. Resolve any issues, especially interpersonal ones, as quickly as possible. Put a policy in place that rewards team members who are able to create resolutions before they become revolutions.

9. Be sure that any criticism is truly constructive. The best way to do that is to remember to be clear and polite. Begin by asking the other person if he would like some input that you think might help him, and be prepared for him to decline your offer. If the other person is your subordinate, she may be hesitant to say no, so let her know that the two of you can talk at another time. It's also wise to make sure that you point to the problem, not at the person.

10. Learn to ask deep questions. Asking in-depth questions at the right time makes a person think, can stop bad behaviors, and gets everyone on the same page. Open-ended questions such as "What is our purpose here?" or "How can we enjoy work and still survive?" have the effect of making a person go beyond thinking of him- or herself and focus on what's best for the team.

These 10 tools are used by the best of the best to make their companies and their team members successful. Once you start the process, the rewards will be obvious.

Resolving Conflicts

The second step in creating an emotionally fit workplace is to create a system of conflict resolution. No matter how great your team may be, eventually someone's toes are going to get stepped on, and you need to have a surefire means of dealing with those types of issues. Learning how to eliminate the negative and accentuate the positive in business may seem trite or even elusive at first glance. Simple cost-effective strategies and applicable techniques can create a successful company, or help a phoenix rise from the ashes.

Learning how to resolve workplace issues requires that you be prepared for them. It will help you deal with overreactions, broken business relationships, and problem-solving. Effective business communication techniques are money and time-savers when you have to deal with difficult people or situations. In today's work environment, we have to learn to be great coaches, get really good at listening, and, when we do have to confront someone, learn how to do it in a caring manner. All of this will make getting through the difficult times much easier.

10 Issue Resolution Preparation Techniques

*Always bear in mind that your own resolution to succeed
is more important than any one thing.*
—Abraham Lincoln

Perhaps the most difficult part of having a deep conversation with someone you work with on a daily basis is getting the process started. Most people open these conversations with little preparation because they can no longer contain their emotions. When this happens sometimes things are said that the speaker may regret afterward. It is wise to think before you talk, especially about issues that may have an emotional charge, so a little internal processing beforehand may be your most valuable tool.

The techniques that follow are specifically designed to help facilitate the necessary thinking required before you talk with your staff or fellow teammates about something that is bothering you. You don't need to use them all; try the ones that are easiest for you and see how they work.

    1. Sleep on it. Forget about it for a while, watch some TV, cook, go fishing—but don't use any of these as an avoidance

technique. This will allow your feelings to settle a little and you'll have a different perspective.

2.   Be sure that the issue is real and you're not just complaining. It's easy to blame someone else when things don't go as planned so check that out before you point a finger. Also look inside yourself and be sure you're not angry about a personal issue that you're projecting on to a teammate.

3.   Think about to whom you're talking. Before you share it, imagine how the person you want to talk to will receive your input. Different people hear things in different ways. If your coworker is visual, perhaps they would respond more favorably to something in writing to get the conversation started. If they are auditory, telling them straight out is best. Just be sure they are not highly sensitive or over reactive.

4.   If appropriate, talk with someone else. Get an objective read on your feelings before you talk to the person you're having the issue with, but don't allow yourself to be overly influenced by someone else's opinion. An objective third party is one of the most underutilized business tools we have at our fingertips.

5.   Write down what you want to say. A pro-and-con list may be the simplest way of deciding what needs to be discussed or even if it's appropriate to have the conversation at all. Read it over before the conversation, because you will want to make some changes after you first write your list. It may also help to take notes on the conversation.

6.   Don't generalize and remember to be prepared with examples. Putting your issues into categories may help you with this. If you have documentation, that is also helpful, but keep it to a manageable level. Don't expect someone to stay focused if you are reading a phone book to him. Strive to cover your points clearly but succinctly.

7.   Don't avoid a possibly painful conversation. Remember that you usually feel better after it's over, and getting started is the hardest part. Once you actually sit down face to face, it may be hard to not just start talking. Also, it can help to keep the finish line in mind.

8. Make an appointment with the person to talk. This can give you the opportunity to get away from your normal routine and have some quiet time to discuss things in an appropriate fashion. Also, be prepared for him or her to say that right now is the best time to talk.

9. Be polite. It's hard to put the toothpaste back in the tube. Venting your anger will only make the gap wider and the issue more clouded. If you are physically or emotionally unbalanced, your ability to behave appropriately will be diminished.

10. Imagine or visualize the conversation. It will help it to go the way you want it to go can see a positive outcome in your mind's eye and allow yourself to feel good about how you'll handle the issue. This is the kind of visualization technique that successful athletes use.

Processing your feelings before you lay them on your team-mate will help you deliver them in the most appropriate manner, and will help your issue resolution discussion go much easier. Once you experience having a positive conversation about a difficult subject, the next ones will not seem as daunting.

Over Reactive People

Those who make peaceful revolution impossible will make violent revolution inevitable.
—John F. Kennedy

When someone steps on your toe, you say, " Ouch!" What do you say and do when someone at the office steps on your emotional toes and hurts your feelings? Saying "ouch" may actually be an appropriate response. Voicing your pain is far better than reacting in a negative way that could end up doing damage to a business relationship that's important to you.

The energy that goes into an overreaction is monumental. Most people are physically and emotionally exhausted after they've "let loose" on someone.

People who instantly react in an aggressive manner generally end up losing their authority and living in fear or with anger. It seems that they are always waiting for the other shoe to drop. What a hard way to go through life!

In order to decide how to respond (rather than react without thinking), you must first consider if the offending action was intentional, what harm was truly done, and if the offender is offering an apology. Whether you are in a new position or one you've had for many years will make a difference in how you feel and how you choose to respond. There are many pieces in play when hurt feelings are flying around the office.

Make no mistake: overreactions are always preceded by some type of emotional pain or perceived fear. Anger should actually be considered a secondary emotion. When you feel it, you need to check out where it's really coming from. If you choose not to and just go into a reactionary rage, you may never get the chance to truly heal the pain.

Learning to catch yourself is the hardest part. When your blood gets boiling, it can be challenging to contain your feelings, but it's worth the effort. If you're having conflict with a team member or client, you will correct it by talking it out rather than just perpetuating it by claming up and holding a grudge.

If you feel yourself getting annoyed or angry at someone, before you "go off," ask yourself if it's really going to get you what you want. Just taking a moment to consider the results is enough to let you simmer down. Hopefully, you will take another path to resolving your pain. I'm not suggesting that you push down your feelings. Rather, instead of erupting, you need to express yourself in a different, more communicative way.

Sometimes it's hard to find the words, and it's okay to put your response on hold for a little while. Perhaps sleeping on it will help you see what it is you really need.

The idea here is to avoid reacting inappropriately when someone with whom (or for whom) you work or for does something that ruffles your feathers. Trust me; it will happen.

Repairing Broken Business Relationships

Do good to your friends to keep them,
to your enemies to win them.
—Benjamin Franklin

Longtime, trusted business relationships are some of the best things we have in the working world. To have someone you've been doing business with successfully for years and is willing to give you an honest opinion (or smack you upside the head) when you need it is a true gift. Here are some tools that will help you repair any damage that may have occurred between you and an old business associate.

- Having to be right or make the other person wrong is not going to work. People who want to work together learn to compromise and consider what's best for each other. Make peace with letting go of your need to win; it's easy when you realize that there's no prize. It may only be stubborn pride that's keeping you isolated from someone who may truly be a valuable ally. If an apology is required, give it or ask for it. How hard is that really? (And it doesn't cost you a thing.) Having a no-fault policy is a great asset in many areas of life, and this is one of them.

- If other people are negatively influencing your business relationships, it is best to first consider the source. There may be competition issues or just personal bad blood. Sometimes individuals who are feeling emotional pain or hurt, project it on to other people. Make your own decisions and ask the deep questions both of yourself and your associates.

- Rebuilding a business relationship is an easy-does-it process. Don't expect to have a conversation or two and then going back to your pervious level. Take some time to get reacquainted; there really isn't a formula for how long, but you should probably spend several weeks talking with your client or coworker to make sure you have a secure understanding of what you want from each other.

- People change, which may be the only thing you can count on. There is always the possibility that you and your associate have outgrown each other. If that is the case, you need to make peace with the situation and move on. There is also the chance the two of you have finally grown up enough to have a truly supportive and profitable business relationship.

- Make allowances for the past, for yourself as well as your associate. If forgiveness from your end is needed, remember that it is a gift you are giving to yourself. No one is perfect, and, in most cases, we hurt or offend people without knowing it. If that's what happened, letting go of one incident and focusing on your years of successful interaction is a potent choice.

So if you have an old business associate who you've been estranged from, take the high road and pick up the phone or send an e-mail, and catch up. You may find that whatever differences pushed you apart will not be as strong as the bond of time that pulls you together. You may be just the person he or she needed to talk to about this new project he or she is working on.

Effective Business Communication

The art of communication is the language of leadership.
—James Humes

To understand how to effectively communicate in the workplace, you have to first understand some basic psychological truths about how we, as people, tend to verbally interact.

If we communicate to a person in the way she understands best, that communication will be accepted and the team member will respond faster and with more motivation. According to research done by Bandler and Grindler, the creators of NLP (Neuro Linguistic Programming), there are three types of communicators. The first are the Visuals, those people who take in and process information through their eyes. They also prefer to think, or rather visualize with their mind's eye. To be effective with them, you need to use key words such as *look*, *see*, *picture*, and so on. It is also valuable to give them printed or written materials to go along with what it is you are communicating. They prefer words that enable them to picture things.

The second type are Auditory communicators. These people use their hearing to develop understanding. They talk to themselves in words that their minds can listen to. They like words that help them hear things. When talking with them, use key words like *hearing, listening, sound*," etc. These people tend to process information quickly and are sometimes likely to respond before you have finished talking.

Kinesthetic, the third type, are feeling people. It doesn't matter how things look or sound to them, it needs to feel right (not necessarily good). Still, others imagine things in terms of movement, feeling, and action. The famous scientist Einstein used this kinesthetic type of thinking when he formulated his famous theory of relativity.

Listen to how your team members communicate. They will use the key words for their type in normal conversation. After you have discovered how they communicate, speak with them in the same manner. It will greatly enhance your interactions.

To gain maximum interest, remember that people are most interested in anything that has to do with them. This isn't egotistical—it's natural. Once you understand this, you can tailor your communications so that you receive maximum interest.

Be aware of non-verbal communications

Our senses shape our thinking. We remember and think about things as we saw, heard, or felt them. Some individuals and cultures stress one kind of thinking more than others do, though all cultures use all of them at one time or another.

You may not be sending the message you intend when dealing across cultures. You may be misinterpreting the sender's message because of cultural differences. It is important to be aware of mixed messages and not make assumptions about the meaning of non-verbal communications.

Many people believe that, when they speak, their words are the primary transporters of their thoughts. That's just not the case. According to research, words can convey as little as 7 percent of communication. Become aware of nonverbal messages to harness your communication power.

Leaning forward and facing someone unconsciously communicates receptiveness and interest. Turning away or staring off into space says you're not really there. In addition, multitasking while someone is trying to talk with you is both disrespectful and unproductive. Chances are you're going to have to have the conversation again because you don't remember everything when you're trying to do two (or more) things at once.

Innovative Problem-Solving

Imagination is more important than knowledge.
—Albert Einstein

The most important function of innovation is to foster the initiative to think beyond the boundaries of what is. The purpose is to promote the kind of thinking that is required to meet the needs of a rapidly changing corporate technology and an even more rapidly changing business marketplace. With innovative thinking, individuals use their state of mind that provides access to their power of creativity.

Leaving the Industrial Age and moving into the Information Age, there is a need to develop different skills. The two most important ones to cultivate are creativity and problem-solving. In the past, many people did much the same jobs in the factories as on the assembly line. In the future, specialization is becoming more and more prevalent; and, in the office, everyone is doing something different. People can no longer depend on the same old answers because the problems are brand new.

The experience of problems

How one experiences problems is a more significant factor in success than are the specific problems themselves. It can be said that life is not about becoming free of problems; rather it is about becoming a better problem-solver. Instead of complaining and worrying, learn to see problems as creative opportunities to grow and improve. Take on problems as puzzles to be solved or as challenges to be overcome.

When one gets into a stressful state, the filter or reticular activating system closes down, denying the individual access to memory and creativity. By utilizing the innovative brain, one can get in touch with his or her problem-solving capabilities. With the filter open, individuals can use the imagination to go beyond what they know and focus on all that could be. This is best done when relaxed, because most people get their best ideas when they're not trying.

Often people who have trouble solving problems are unable to see the problem for what it truly is. This is the "you can't see the forest for the trees" syndrome. People caught up in the emotions sometimes blow the problem all out of proportion. It helps if people are able to create an alternate perception and see the problem in a different way. Step outside of the problem, change perception, and the problem seems to change.

Creative problem-solving techniques

Imagine the problem belongs to someone else. If this were true, what kind of advice would you give them? What would you say their first step should be? How would you help to motivate them and get them going? What resources would you suggest that they utilize? How can you help them become more confident of their process and their ultimate success?

Alternatively, pretend that the problem is already solved. Think backward from the solution to the first step. Remember how you did it. Where were you when you figured it out, and what were you doing? Realize how good it feels to have it solved. Be proud of yourself. Sometimes people can solve a problem simply by realizing that it is not really a problem at all.

Many problems can be seen in a positive light, as creative opportunities to exercise one's minds and talents to create some positive change. For every problem there are solutions, though some are better than others. One of the most limiting forms of thinking is to assume that there is only one right answer to a specific problem. This rigid and restrictive thinking process comes from the inflexible and limiting experience most students have in our educational system. In school, kids are generally taught that there is only one right answer, and anything else is wrong. In order to become truly effective problem-solvers, that mold needs to be broken. People who can relax their minds and use their imagination and creativity will find unlimited resources at their disposal.

Using a different intelligence

Almost all of the great problems solved had their solutions initially emanate from someone's daydream. It is the daydream state, the alpha brainwave state, where most great ideas are born. One little clue or creative idea is all that it takes to begin solving the most perplexing problems. This type of innovative thinking is a great tool to help get in touch with the imagination. It is a wonderful technique to improve the capacity for problem solving and to enhance creativity. It is a little like creating new software for the mind. The mind can be programmed to help solve problems, and to enhance insight, intuition, and inspiration. All an individual has to do to access this part of the brain is relax. Don't force creativity; coax it. Mindless activities such as exercise, driving, and even watching television are great idea-generators. Many people get their best ideas in the shower or just as they fall asleep. The key is to get into the right state of mind—the state of relaxation.

For many people relaxation is not easy; however, here are two techniques that work well for most individuals.

- Tense/Release: Tighten all the muscles in the body for several seconds and then release the tension. Do this three times, and after the third let the body and mind relax. Allow the mind to flow freely, to seek its own answers.

- Mini Vacation: Imagine that you are in Hawaii for a minute or two. Feel the sun on your face, your toes in the sand, and the wind in your hair. Let the tension leave your mind and body. Ideas will flow to you like gentle waves.

Positive results

Solving even the most difficult problems does not require tension and stress. In fact, intensity often prevents people from experiencing problem resolution. When one gets in touch with his/her intuition, creating new ideas is easy. People who believe in this perspective and practice it generally find it easier to identify the answers they need.

Thomas Edison understood and utilized this concept. After much frustration (more than 1,000 failures) in trying to invent the light bulb, Edison decided to try a different approach, instead of brainstorming or continuing with his experiments. As I mentioned earlier, he took lots of naps. He did this because he got great ideas while dreaming. In this particular dream, he got the idea to coat the bulb filaments with carbon, and developed the incandescent lamp. He allowed his imagination to do the work for him, while he was sleeping! He knew how to access his imagination and he knew that stressing to find a solution was not the answer. So the next time you are faced with solving a problem, remember that relaxation opens the door and imagination primes the pump.

Difficult People in the Workplace

*If the only tool you have is a hammer, you treat
everything like a nail.*
—Abraham Maslow

We all encounter difficult people every day. Sometimes all we have to do to see one is to look in the mirror. Is there a person in your life or business who is demanding and intimidating? What about the person who never follows through or who is never happy? If you have to deal with a difficult person, here are some surefire methods for understanding and communicating with them.

If someone is aggressive or intimidating in his or her manner, there are a couple of tactics that work well. First, listen to what it is he or she has to say, but don't engage in an argument. Being polite, succinct, and precise in your language will give the person less room to engage in this negative behavior. If the person makes you nervous (which he or she does to control the situation) it may be wise to have someone else in the room when you are talking with him or her.

If the person criticizes you or pelts you with sarcastic comments that offend you, keep the conversation focused on the solution and don't acknowledge the inappropriateness. In cases like this it gives you more power if you remember to act rather than to react. Don't play the game, as he or she are trying to make you feel unstable. In a difficult conversation, the first person to get mad loses.

When dealing with a person who is cold and closed off, you need to consider that he may have a hidden agenda. Ask open-ended questions and be patient; it may take a little while but he will open up when he feels safe.

Perhaps one of the most difficult people to deal with is someone who is egotistical. People who engage in this behavior are usually trying to cover up their own insecurity. They may be trying to avoid taking responsibility for a problem which will be made obvious if they try to blame others. Dealing with them effectively requires that you know you're in the right. It also helps to have documentation to back up your observations.

When someone continually complains it can bring down an entire group of people and perhaps even a company. This kind of cynicism is uncomfortable for everyone around this person. The best way to deal with it is to not allow the person to complain unless she also presents a solution to the issue. This will greatly reduce her ability to affect you and her fellow team members.

Some people talk so much that they are unable to hear anyone else. A great technique is to tell them as they begin that you only have a minute. If they continue bending your ear, don't be afraid to interrupt and say that you (and him or her) have to get back to what you were doing when the conversation began.

If someone is not doing his or her fair share around the office, it can be very frustrating. These people can put more effort into finding shortcuts than what it would take to just do the job. Don't cover for them, that's what they want you to do. If they ask for help or advice, have them create a list of what it is they need to accomplish. People who are prone to procrastinating are also usually unfocused and disorganized. To deal with them, set firm time lines and emphasize the importance of meeting them. Be sure they know there are consequences if the time lines are not met. This will help to eliminate any excuses that they can think of. Be sure they give you a firm commitment and follow-up weekly.

Finally, some people hold on to every negative thing that has ever happened. They are not good team players and tend to work best in isolation. Take the pre-emptive approach with them; before you start, clarify that you are not present to rehash old conflicts. If past conflicts begin to surface cut the person off quickly and return to the issue at hand.

Sometimes we cannot deal with difficult types and we must move them on (or move on yourself). Life is too short to work (or hang out) with people who make you miserable. One of the best tools for keeping a team together is making sure they get along. If the problem persists, you may want to rethink your motivation for continuing to work with someone who behaves in a difficult manner.

Dealing with difficult people is an art form. Those who are good at it tend to be successful in life and business (or they become consultants). Knowing how someone is likely to behave is helpful, and will give you the upper hand in an uncomfortable situation. Trust your instincts and don't let them grind you down.

Saying the Wrong Thing

How often misused words generate misleading thoughts.
—Herbert Spencer

Leaders have to speak to individuals and groups more than most. And because we are all human, it is not uncommon that, upon occasion, we can say the wrong thing at the wrong time, to the wrong person. Sometimes, it embarrasses us. When we try to cover up our embarrassment with righteous indignation, a real problem can begin. The truth is, to resolve the problem, we have to take responsibility for creating the energy that caused the upset, and that can be difficult at first.

Sometimes, when we have said the wrong thing and have hurt someone on our team, we may want to or try to believe that we were helpless to prevent it. We can feel that we have been provoked, and our staff member's behavior is to blame for causing us to say the wrong thing, overreact, cast blame, or just be downright rude. Some in charge have been conditioned to be harsh; others mistakenly believe that they have a right to behave this way. And most unfortunately, some actually enjoy going off on team members.

To understand this, there are two issues to consider. First, how could you (or your company) have created the culture to allow your people to behave in this unproductive manner? For example, did you get your initial leadership training or experience from a company that encouraged management by intimidation? If so, then you may have been taught that this kind of projection is reasonable. Second, are you willing to assign the role of a victim to your team members (or yourself)? You have the choice to cast away any thoughts of lashing out and get to the real problem (which may actually be you). To let go of the roles we have become used to and to choose a new experience is the wisest choice to make, but it isn't easy.

To avoid reinforcing false beliefs that someone other than yourself is responsible for the problem (or for your behavior), don't wait. When you first realize that you have said the wrong thing, stop and apologize. Besides, waiting too long to remedy the situation can cause resentments to build in your company and that will affect the bottom line.

If your behavior happens because you feel exhausted, then you need to rest and recuperate; learn to take care of yourself. If it's been a hard day, then you need to learn to ask appropriate questions, not snarl, grumble, and try to make your team member feel as bad as you do. That creates a win/lose scenario rather than a win/win situation.

If you feel your team member has done something that was incorrect, it is appropriate to take immediate action and respond. The correct method is to look at the person and say directly (and kindly) what is on your mind or what problems you see occurring from his or her behaviors.

It can't be fixed if it isn't shared. Your team member, upon realizing that the behavior is inappropriate, should choose the necessary steps to rectify the situation. A little mentoring here may also be a good idea.

Although it is best, it isn't necessary to get an immediate response. Some people need a little time to process their feelings. An hour is the average time it takes for most people to calm down and realize what it is they need to do. If much more time is necessary, or if days go by without the situation being rectified, it may be time to discuss the matter with a third party.

Taking responsibility for mistaken words and doing what is necessary to correct the situation is a sign of a great leader. In addition to making you feel good about yourself and strengthening your character, it will also strengthen your business.

Resolving Issues at Work

*It is always during a passing state of mind that
we make lasting resolutions.*
—Marcel Proust

I have walked into offices where you could feel the negative
energy—it was literally palpable. Team members may have difficulty expressing their feelings appropriately to others in the workplace if there is not a forum for doing so.

Joe Phelps, CEO of the Phelps Group and author of the book
Pyramids Are Tombs has a method that has kept his company
humming, his profits up, and his turnover low. They don't believe
in rules at the Phelps Group, and they only hire adults so there is
no need to tell people how to behave. Instead, Joe encourages his
team members who have an issue with someone else in the company to approach that person and deal directly with him or her. If
that doesn't work, they then bring in two other team members
who know both of the people involved and try to work things out.
If necessary, as a final step, someone outside the team can be
brought in to facilitate a resolution.

I believe that if team members took a little time to think first, most issues would never be brought to the table. The following are 10 questions leaders and team members need to ask themselves before taking an issue with a coworker or supervisor to the next level.

Issue-Resolution Questions

Ask yourself:

1. What do I need to resolve in this conversation?
2. Have I, in some way, contributed to this issue?
3. Are either of us trying to avoid responsibility?
4. Am I really upset about this, or is it something else?
5. What was the genesis for this difficulty?
6. Can we avoid issues like this in the future?
7. Is this the right time to bring the issue up?
8. Would I be better off just letting this go?
9. Should I take this to HR or bring in a third party?
10. What does taking the high road look like in this case?

The previous questions are specifically designed to facilitate and assist businesspeople in dealing with their coworkers when an issue takes on an emotional charge. Take the time to think before you act, and that means in e-mail, too.

So ask yourself the appropriate questions, think first, and consider which of the ones above will be most helpful to you and your team. When an issue is presented, immediately make an appointment to talk about it. Letting it fester will cause your productivity to decline because your mind won't be on your work. So initiate the conversation sooner rather than later.

These questions and techniques are also very helpful when dealing with customer and client problems. Issues happen daily, it's how we receive and resolve them that separates the successful companies from the rest.

Speed Bumps on the Road to Success

*A great secret of success is to go through life as
a man who never gets used up.*
—Albert Schweitzer

I believe that any disagreement can be turned into a positive experience. I call these experiences "speed bumps" because they require us to slow down and look at the circumstances and behaviors that surround our issues at work. Slowing down is important because, if you don't, the issue (speed bump) is going to rattle you and you won't be able to respond appropriately.

For most, these uncomfortable moments are really opportunities for growth. If they are overlooked you are left with the same behaviors that caused the upset. If you utilize the moment to focus on resolving the issue appropriately, without raised voices or saying things that will anger one another, everyone involved and the business will grow. Furthermore, you will not have to drive over the same rough road time and time again.

Learning to slow down and look at your actions, take corrective measures, and agree on the best way to proceed is not easy at first. Begin by recognizing that you have hit a speed bump and that you need to use it to make things better. That step alone will keep the situation from escalating into a multi-car pileup.

Once you have agreed that you are going to work this through in a safe and sane manner then simply replay your version of what happened between you and your coworker. This way you both know what the other person experienced and how he or she are feeling. You can then respond to his or her needs rather than react to your own highly charged emotions.

Now you need to take a little time to process what has occurred. For most people an hour is enough but others may need much less or a little more time. It all depends on your experience; individuals who know how to use speed bumps as a growth opportunity need much less time to process their feelings than those who are new at it. Whatever the length of time that is needed you must agree to never walk away angry with the other person. If that means talking about it into the wee hours of the morning, so be it. Truth be told, if you don't resolve the issue you won't be your best self the next day—no matter how much sleep you get.

Once you have experienced what it is like to actually resolve an issue with a coworker or boss, you will be more available to do it again the next time. You will also have the benefit of not holding on to the negative feelings that accompany arguments. Correctly processing and communicating your feelings are two of the best tools you have for maintaining a profitable business and for keeping your job.

Everyone experiences difficult moments. It is how we handle these moments that make the difference between businesses that work and those that don't. Slowly and calmly investigating the way you deal with problems is a tool that will make your working world a better, and more successful, place to be.

So the next time you hit a speed bump, slow yourself down and take a little time to examine how you really feel about what has occurred. It could be the moment that prevents your company from becoming a car wreck and turns it into an Indy 500 (or Fortune 100) winner. See you at the finish line.

Leader or Dictator?

A leader has been defined as one who knows the way, goes the way, and shows the way.
—Anonymous

Releasing the need to control is a technique that only the most successful of business people have mastered. Allowing your team members to follow their own ideas and inspirations will give your company a leg-up on the competition and fosters an atmosphere of creativity.

Most people resist or rebel when someone with whom they work is overbearing or controlling. They will cease to contribute in a positive manner and create a wall of emotional protection around themselves. In addition, if someone's ideas for improvements are ignored, that person may no longer offer up his or her insights, and that could be a fatal loss.

To circumvent having one of your valued team members pull back, teams and leaders need to examine how they deliver assignments and discuss duties with one another. What one person says may not be what the other hears.

This is not a difficult procedure and won't get in the way of motivating your team to get the job done. On the contrary, it will only help because having this understanding and being able to tell someone what you need and expect in a way they will hear it will serve to keep your company and department moving forward.

Giving someone a direct (and perhaps harsh) order is just not the best way to motivate him or her. If you really want to succeed you have to learn how to psychologically inspire others to do their best. It also encourages open communication and great brainstorming because your team members will feel like their ideas are respected. Without open communication and brainstorming, you are eventually going to lose business.

Acting out by yelling, withholding recognition, or just being nasty is a losing game. It will never help you get what you want. In truth, it will only serve to alienate your team. If you think this behavior is okay, I implore you to ask your staff members what they are experiencing. It may feel a tad bit uncomfortable, but if you do it now, you'll save yourself a lot of grief in the future.

Having a team that works well together is going to get you far. If your team is at odds with one another or with you it will not help you achieve the desired results. Try pulling back on your "commander" and being more of a coach. You are in control. All you have to do is make a few minor adjustments in how you ask for what is needed.

This is an area of business where the Golden Rule makes complete sense. Just treating your team in the way you like to be treated can solve many issues. This is not rocket science, but it's a discovery that could shoot your business to the moon.

23
The Art of Successful Listening

No one ever listened themselves out of a job.
—Calvin Coolidge

Listening is the key to understanding what is going on in a person's mind. One of the things that makes great leaders successful is because, no matter with whom he or she is speaking, the great leader is able to make that person feel that he or she was the only one in the room.

Imagine how it would make your boss or coworker feel if you gave her or him 100 percent of your attention while he or she was talking to you. Imagine how you would feel if you got the same kind of focus from your team or managers. This one act alone can turn conflict into cooperation and turn your business relationships from pain to pleasure.

When companies first hire a communications consultant, most will state that their team's inattention is one of their major issues. As the whole company learns communication skills, all parties become aware of how they haven't listened. They also experience the difference between focused listening, where you give 100 percent of your attention versus selective listening. This is where one person or the other has gotten skilled at pretending he or she listening but are really just looking in the direction of where the words are coming from.

You don't need to bring in a pro to develop good listening skills; there are many excellent books, Websites, and DVDs on the subject. There is also the common sense approach, which includes learning how and why you currently listen selectively and what you need to do to correct the problem.

There are three different ways you can listen so that your coworker really gets that you are tuned into what it is they are communicating:

1. Active listening.
2 Reflective listening.
3. Empathetic listening.

Active listening when you ask open-ended questions about what it is your coworker has said, such as "Tell me more about what it was that upset you" or "How did that make you feel?"

The second type of listening is called *reflective listening,* which is accomplished by paraphrasing or even repeating what it is your teammate has said. For example, if he or she is talking about something that irritated him or her, your response should be something like "What I'm hearing is that it really bugged the hell out of you."

The third type of listening is *empathetic listening,* which you do by tuning into and saying out loud the feeling behind what your staff member or boss has said, such as "You sound very angry because of what happened." This kind of listening validates a person's emotions and makes him feel that someone has heard him completely. When a person feels that someone in power really gets it, she is less likely to have to rehash the issue, and it makes the company stronger because the issues won't take up valuable time or create distance between two (or more) team members. It puts people on the same emotional wavelength.

Listening skills are essential to emotionally fit businesses. They will help your company players understand each other's needs and motivations, and that will create deeper respect and appreciation.

They also give you the added benefit of defusing anger and keep resentments from growing into business breaking arguments.

Learning to listen deeply is a skill that all companies need to develop and keep refining as they and their businesses mature. There are no guarantees of success in this economy, but learning how to make your team members feel that you are listening to what they say can be seen as a long term warranty for your company's success.

Carefrontation

No one cares how much you know, until they know how much you care.
—Anonymous

In successful and emotionally balanced companies, the people working in them discuss things, no matter how bad they've gotten. They don't run and hide, they don't name call, and they don't put their foot down. They are willing and able to talk without rancor and in a straightforward manner about what is bothering them. I call this process Carefrontation. It is a made-up word that is a combination of caring and confrontation. The spirit behind it is that everyone involved in the business wants it to grow and continue improve and for everyone to prosper and enjoy the work.

Being Carefrontational requires being willing to take a risk and to be understanding of the person you are talking to. If you are not willing to share something that is bothering you with your teammates, then your working relationship will be diminished. In addition, those who withhold their emotions and ideas cease to grow, or, worse, grow away from the company. If you cannot share your feelings in a Carefrontational manner, the people you work with may not be able to absorb the information they are given. So this is an important skill to master and a very valuable tool to those on your team.

Creative and successful people want to find balance in their working relationships without feeling angry and misunderstood. And sometimes that's very hard. Because confronting someone you work with on a daily basis with a challenging issue is not easy, it is best to start simply with willingness. Sometimes, just being willing to be willing is enough. Willingness will help you to share your feelings in a Carefrontational way, and will make the words easier to find and to hear.

When a working relationship is in distress, the truth is sometimes hidden. In order to find the real answers, everyone involved has to be willing to be rigorously honest with themselves and with each other. This is not an easy step because it almost always brings up uncomfortable feelings. Knowing that you have the agreement of Carefrontation in your business will make it safer for you to say what you need to because you know your team is committed to hearing your feelings in an appropriate manner. Learning to present and respond to feelings in this way is what allows successful companies to make it through difficult times.

Leaders who want their business to survive the downturn must be willing to take the risk of seeking the real truth, in a Carefrontational manner, even if it means that they're not in the right. Maintaining this attitude will help companies achieve prosperity and build a team that will stand the test of time and the turmoil that the world has dropped on our doorstep.

Carefrontation is not just a made-up word; it's an attitude that takes its roots in wanting to be part of a successful working relationship that has a spirit of commitment. If you never want to grow or hate the idea of change your company may ripen, but it will eventually rot. To keep your business green and growing, commit to telling your teammates anything and everything in a Carefrontational manner.

10 Ways We Can Work It Out

If you have learned how to disagree without being disagreeable, then you have discovered the secret of getting along.
—Bernard Meltzer

The Beatles were still in their 20s when they wrote "We Can Work It Out," but somehow they understood that, even though resolving issues can be hard, it is better than trashing a business relationship, a job or a deal. Here are 10 tips to help you work things out.

1. When you're having a difficult discussion, put your anger aside. You can't be logical when you're mad. If you can't contain your ire, it may be best to put talking on hold until after you calm down. Take a walk, recheck your e-mail, or talk to a trusted coworker, but wait until you're stable before you have the conversation.

2. It's not about who's right or wrong. If you try to blame your coworker/client or make him or her wrong, you won't find an answer. You both have to take responsibility for getting things back on a positive track. Great thing is that just by taking this attitude, you're halfway to a resolution.

3. Look for the high road and discuss what's best for everyone concerned. Don't settle for anything less than equality and the knowledge that you are doing the right thing for yourself, your teammates and your clients. In many cases win/lose is the same as lose/lose. Try and make everyone come out a winner.

4. Be humble and don't rub your someone's nose in a misstep. If you share your feelings with a dash of kindness, whomever is the offending party will learn from his or her mistake much easier. It also helps to ask the person how they might have done it differently or what still needs to be handled.

5. You can agree to disagree. But don't settle for less than a complete acceptance of each other's point of view. If you walk away disappointed, you have not resolved your issue. For a business relationship to work, you both have to feel like you have each other's support. If you need to compromise, be okay with it. It's probably better than killing the deal, the messenger, or yourself.

6. Always have difficult conversations in private. You don't want others to pick up the negativity; it can make them feel insecure about your performance ability. Remember that you can be heard behind closed doors, so keep the volume low and the vibe as calm as possible.

7. Make sure you consider all of your options. This requires some brainstorming and working together to create a positive solution. If done correctly, this process alone can heal the difficulty. And it needs to be done before making any decision about how to handle a problem.

8. Don't rush to judgment. You may not be able to come up with the best answers in the moment, so sleep on it before you decide on a course of action. If you still cannot reach a meeting of the minds, put the issue aside and look at it again in a day or two.

9. Trust that you can find an answer that will work for everyone. Going into the discussion with an optimistic heart and mind will make working it out much easier. Keep talking. As

long as you are engaged in a conversation, you can create a reasonable result for all concerned.

10. Consolidate the gains of your discussion. Talk about what worked and what didn't. Review out loud what you agreed upon, put it in writing if you like, and then move on. Remember that, once you say you are done, you have to let the issue go.

Most people avoid difficult conversations because they fear having an uncomfortable moment. I think a bad few minutes is better than an uncomfortable work-life. Truth is that those who are able to work things out have more successful careers.

Working Well With Others

Step 3 offers tools to assist workers, managers and leaders alike in identifying how positive thinking and interpersonal actions can help a company grow. From something as simple as keeping your word or apologizing for saying the wrong thing (something we all do), will help anyone in business turn lemons into lemonade. Getting caught up in what others may think, blaming, shaming or complaining, and not being willing to compromise will keep you from reaching your goals. Learning to treat your fellow team members appropriately and respectfully, and avoiding withholding things that need to be said will lift you and your team to the next level. And all of this happens by taking small, easy-to-implement steps.

Keeping Your Word

One thing you can give and still keep is your word.
—Anonymous

Trust is one of the key building blocks for any professional relationship. Each time we keep our word it strengthens the bridge between us and whomever we're working with. Here are 10 tools to help you create and maintain a healthy foundation of honesty.

1. Follow through. These are two of the most important words when it comes to communication and success. If you say you're going to do something and then don't do it, you are creating trust issues with the person or company you're not showing up for.

2. When you don't keep your word, it diminishes your value to your coworkers. It will make your clients think that you don't care about their business and make your team members take everything you say with a grain of salt. People will remember that they were not that important to you and carry that around for a long while.

105

3. Explain why you can't do something. If you have a good reason for not keeping your word (a medical issue, accident, and so on), share it with the parties concerned as soon as possible. Give other people a chance to change their plans and make appropriate adjustments. It's just common courtesy.

4. You have the right to change your mind. If you said you would do something and later regret making that decision, that's okay. However, be sure that you are changing your mind for the right reasons and not just out of laziness or because a better offer has come your way.

5. Are you just forgetful? Could you be having memory issues? If so, you must talk to a physician and make sure your overall health is good. Some people who tend to be forgetful lead long, healthy lives; others may have serious medical conditions that make them forget. Best to get it checked out.

6. Be okay with being reminded. If you are forgetful by nature, tell your coworkers, clients, and friends that it's okay for them to remind you about commitments, and don't take it personally when they do.

7. Access your promise quotient. Do you over-promise and under-deliver? Do you try to do too much? Do you say yes before you've given yourself a chance to realize what you're getting in to? Think about the times you didn't keep your word and ask yourself why and promise yourself you'll never do it again.

8. Don't write a check with your mouth that your head can't cash. Perhaps the biggest crime in this arena is telling someone you want to work with them when you really don't. If your attitude about a client or team member has changed, let him or her know in a kind way and offer closure (which means that you talk about it).

9. How do you feel about yourself? When you break your word, the fallout can have a profound effect on you. It may cause you to think of yourself as a dishonest person and lower your self-esteem, which reduces your effectiveness.

10. Don't be a show-off. If you're trying to impress someone and you make an offer that you really can't afford. Following

through may cost you money and time, but it will serve as a reminder for you to not try to be such a big shot.

Honoring all your commitments is one of those gifts you actually give to yourself. If you make a promise, keep it, no matter what. The positive results will be reflected in your company's bottom line and in your self-worth.

When Life (or the Economy) Hands You Lemons

He knows not his own strength that hath not met adversity.
—Ben Johnson

Sometimes business just doesn't go right. It may be the financial climate, the team, or, perhaps, the alignment of the planets. Whatever the reason, your systems just start to unravel and it may seem like you and your company will never be the same again.

Perhaps you are feeling overwhelming anxiety in the pit of your stomach. Maybe your thoughts are racing and you just can't find any peace of mind. You've lost your optimism, and, even if you saw a light at the end of the tunnel, it would probably be an oncoming train.

At this point, you need to get a grip and realize that this is a low time or a slow time, which you may have to endure for a while. Challenging situations can cause us to withdraw or to make us want to put the responsibility for fixing things on someone else. The real truth is that, whether we are a team member or a leader, we have to choose to step up when the situation calls for it and not give into our emotional fears.

Dealing with the lows and slows isn't easy or fun. Teammates try to make you smile, and all you want to do is leave the room. TV shows or articles about successful people or companies make you cringe, and there's just no joy to be found in Muddville.

Times like these are called *situational depressions*; all businesses and people go through them. The pain for some is palpable. For others, it is just a blah time, where you can't notice the beauty of a sunset or imagine the thought of a successful conclusion. These are the times that try our souls. They are also the times that forge our characters and teach us the value of appreciating what we have built.

I suggest you give your own natural defenses a chance to rally to your cause. Start by watching your diet and exercise. Try to keep those two things stable, so you have the strength to deal with your situation. It's also wise to listen to friends if they tell you that you're not taking good enough care of yourself. Hearing it from someone you trust is going to make a difference. Time off may also be an option.

Next, I recommend a little biblio-therapy; read something that can give you a dose of inspiration. Not to minimize your situation at all, but millions of people have gotten through their dark times and been better for it. You have to make a choice here not to give in to the desire to do nothing. Even going to a seminar or running an errand for your business is better than sitting in your own stress.

That being said, it's also important to let the hurt out. Holding it in can lead to a major depression, which is something you want to avoid. Once you've been there, it becomes easier to go back. So force yourself to go on with your day, talk to a least one sympathetic coworker, and share your troubles. It's also important to let out your pain by writing or talking so you can make room for positive feelings to emerge.

It is estimated that depression costs American business $70 billion a year. Your job is to make sure that it doesn't cost you your job or your company. If your business is going through a major transition you might want to consider bringing in a professional counselor to help your team rally their forces.

Take heart. With a little time you will feel like yourself again, your company will be back in the black, and you may actually be wiser for having gone through the experience.

What Others Think

For every action, there is an equal and opposite criticism.
—Anonymous

The time you spend dwelling on what others think of you is time taken away from your business and the good things in life. When someone is concerned about what other people may be thinking of them, I always like to relate a story from what I have come to call "the B files."

Many years ago, I went through a relationship breakup in the middle of a professional convention. As I negotiated terms with my soon-to-be ex on the mezzanine level of some long-ago forgotten hotel, she looked at me and asked, "Aren't you embarrassed doing this in front of all these people?" I scanned the room and replied with a smile, saying, "Everyone here is so self-absorbed, they're never going to remember anything we do." I returned to the same conference for several years, and no one ever mentioned it, or her, to me.

The truth is that people really don't have enough room in their heads to keep track of the petty foibles you may have perpetrated in their presence. Most of our fears about what others think about us really comes from our own insecurities.

If you are a person who tends to judge or compare yourself with others while trying to keep up with the Joneses, you may just be reflecting your own thoughts. A lot of people believe that others think the same way they do, and most of the time that just isn't the case.

We are all pretty wrapped up in our own lives, be they soap operas, comedies, or pseudo-reality shows. Our attention is more focused on ourselves than on what someone else may be doing. At times, people may think about the lives of others much for the same reason they watch television or read a good mystery: it helps them to escape from their own troubles for a little while.

Yes, your clients and coworkers may be chatting or even gossiping about your hair transplant. There may even be wild speculation about the origin of the donor hairs. But, think about it. How much time do you devote to staying tuned into the multitude of mini-dramas that surround you?

Unless you do something heinous or hurtful, the people you work with are not going to hang on to your missteps nearly as long as you will. In addition, if someone is judging you because you didn't have it together for a moment or two, you have to ask yourself if that person is really worth working with.

So, stop worrying about what other people may think of you. Go ahead and present that "off the wall" proposal, start your new business, or take that trip down the Amazon with your tax refund. It's been my experience that, if you're a relatively decent human being and you have a sense of humor about yourself, people usually remember the best parts about you.

Don't Blame, Shame, or Complain

Criticism of others is futile and if you indulge in it often you should be warned that it can be fatal to your career.
—Dale Carnegie

Communicating to a team member can be more dependent on how you say it rather than what it is you say. If you blame, shame, or complain, your teammate could get defensive and not be able to take in what it is you are trying to tell him or her.

When someone feels blamed, he or she can immediately go into denial about what you are trying to share. For many people, feeling blamed takes them right back to childhood and they will choose to ignore the problem, get over-sensitive, or become angry. Telling a staff member how you feel without blaming will help engage him or her in resolving the issue rather than confusing it or having things escalate into an argument.

Blaming is also a way of avoiding responsibility. Making any issue someone else's fault takes away the opportunity you have to correct a negative action and grow from the experience. If you want to be the team member and person you can, own your behaviors. It is also wise to remember that there are such things as honest mistakes, and, for those, doing everything you can to resolve the problem is the key.

Shaming someone is one of the most ineffective and destructive means of getting your way or avoiding an issue. I actually think it borders on emotional abuse. When a person feels shamed he or she becomes disempowered and is no longer participating in the discussion. The shamed individual is emotionally processing feelings of guilt and not being good enough instead of looking to solve a problem. People who work with others who are shaming feel weak and are not able to give their teams the finest parts of themselves.

Shaming behavior can include name-calling, belittling, bullying, comparing one person to another, or using foul language. Treating a team member in this way will not get you what you want; it will only serve to further alienate him or her from you. If you are hurt or angry with a teammate, tell him or her so without adding fuel to the fire. A straightforward approach will help you accomplish so much more than a shaming or negative remark will.

Complaints are universal in life, but how you complain can be the difference between a caring teammate and one who could care less. Letting your team members know that changes are needed is an important part of a healthy working relationship. Doing it without anger or attitude is the sign of a mature leader.

Explaining how your teammate's behaviors make you uncomfortable and how he or she could do things differently is far more effective than just harping about what seems wrong or raising your voice to get your point across. Most people are receptive to gentle, positive suggestions. If you haven't tried it in a while give it a shot. You may be surprised at how well a little tact works.

Blaming, shaming, and complaining are ineffective tools when it comes to building a positive working environment. Put them away and use your best communication cornerstones instead.

Are You an Innovator or an Implementer?

The main thing is to keep the main thing the main thing.
—Albert Einstein

Innovation cannot exist without implementation. To foster new ideas or sometimes just to keep your head above water, it is necessary to get inventive, which comes from the core of creativity: our emotions. But to put those ideas into practice, you must implement them. Having your teams balanced with both innovators and implementers is the only way to truly solve problems, create new products or services, and, most importantly, succeed.

We often confuse creative ability with artistic ability. We believe truly creative people are those we see on the big screen, created the paintings that hang on museum walls, wrote a best-seller, and even made it to the American Idol top 10. This is a serious misconception. We also forget about all the work done behind the scenes (by the implememters) that makes the final result look so easy.

We each have creative ability. Have you enjoyed the experience of witnessing an auto mechanic who makes your car sing? Or the surgeon who operates with the intuitive ability of Michelangelo? We have the ability to take our work, our companies, and lift them to new levels, to those of an art form. We have all seen the most creative geniuses as work—they are creative investors, marketing gurus, research and development specialists. Have you ever needed an extremely creative accountant?

Creativity involves using our emotions and our brains to change, renew, and recombine aspects of our lives. Creativity involves using our sixth sense, or intuition, to perceive the world and make use of our discoveries.

We are often afraid to try new ideas, as we develop attitudes about creativity that can keep us stuck in our world of safety—attitudes like: *It's not important. I don't have time. I already have the answer. I'm not creative.* These cause us to miss opportunities that we find in an ever-changing world. When we become stuck, we run the risk of being quickly left behind.

What are we to do if we are not naturally gifted with creativity and intuitive ability? I believe that intuition comes from a part of the mind that brings ideas to consciousness. When we are in touch with our intuition, we are given a gift in being able to sense trends, danger, and potential problems. It's an unspoken dialogue within ourselves that serves us well, when we learn to trust it. Most of us have had the experience of "not listening to our gut." We would have been better off if we had. Intuition points us in the direction we need to follow. Our intuition takes place when we are in touch with ourselves. We know it is working when things make sense all of a sudden—memories, fantasies, and the sixth sense we pick up from other people.

The issue with creativity is not always knowing the right answers, but knowing the right questions. As a leader, it is not our job to have the answers. It is our job to question the answers. This is tough for most businesspeople to accept. Because of our personalities we rarely display the patience to coach our people. It is far easier and quicker to give them the answers.

The Goldsmith Innovation/Implementation Index (g3i) determines how innovative we are and how well we implement. The personalities with the strongest levels of creativity are often those who are inflexible and do not deal with others very well. Ludwig von Beethoven, Thomas Edison, and Winston Churchill are all examples of those who have tremendous creativity; just don't expect them to be warm, friendly, accommodating, and cooperative. Creative people have a vision in mind; their difficulty is expressing it to others. They frustrate themselves, as well as others, with their inability to effectively communicate.

The advantages and disadvantages of both "Innovators" and "Implementers" are equally weighted. Each is capable of running a business and creating wealth, but those with higher scores tend to be less able to work for someone else. What we have seen with the thousands of executives, managers, and staff who have taken this survey is that those with higher scores tend to be in startup and riskier businesses or investments. Those with lower scores tend to be in corporate positions or family businesses and are more conservative investors. The entrepreneur tends to be more innovative than a corporate CEO. These results could be a predisposition (nature) or a result of personal experiences (nurture). The ability to learn and apply new thinking is more of an innovative process, whereas the ability to learn and apply new tasks is more of an Implementer. High Innovators tend to have more disadvantages and advantages than high Implementers do—this means that Innovators have a more complex personality than Implementers. They tend to have more traits, both better and worse. Other notable differences are that Implementers have the ability to attend to detail in ways that Innovators sometimes find impossible. Also, the incidence of Attention Deficit Disorder (ADD) is much higher in Innovators than Implementers, at a ratio of eight to one. This sub group also tended to be the most successful entrepreneurs, as most had two or more income streams or businesses. The Innovators also confessed to being B/C students, where the Implementers were A/B students, most likely because of their ability to deal with detail.

If you would like to find out if you are an Innovator or an Implementer, the g3i is available for free on my Website at *www.BartonGoldsmith.com*.

The Art of Compromise

There is only one boss—the customer. And he can fire everybody in the company from the chairman on down, simply by spending his money somewhere else.
—Sam Walton

Compromise may be the most important and most underused word in modern business.

Webster defines compromise as a settlement of differences by consent, reached by mutual concessions. Put in simple terms, you've got to give a little to get a little, with the understanding that, just because you don't get what you want, doesn't mean you won't get all you need. For a business to be successful, leaders and team members need to learn how to engage in this beneficial behavior. And it's not as hard as you might think.

The first thing to remember is that, in a business deal, you won't be comfortable unless the other company (or person) is comfortable as well. For some reason compromising can be looked at as a loss, caving in, or even being a doormat. The real truth is that if you have any of these sensations you are not really compromising. For there to be a real meeting of the minds both people have to feel good about the end result.

Getting everything you want every time you want it is not real-istic. Those are the desires of a spoiled child, not an adult who wants to be in a successful business environment. Ask yourself: If you get everything you want, and your client is feeling like he got the fuzzy end of the lollipop (and not at all happy about it) can you really see this deal being successful? Do you think this client will be back for more?

To become willing to compromise you have to understand that it benefits everyone involved. If you are truly business partners then what is good for one should be good for the other. Try looking at the big picture and do what you can to make it balanced. The closer you come to equality the more successful both of you will be. If either one of you feel that the deal is unbalanced, then some-thing isn't working properly.

Once you've agreed to a set of ground rules for your business relationship, if one of you decides to make drastic changes (for example, you or your client want to change the financial terms), it can make future negotiations difficult. Before you do anything that changes the foundation of your agreements, you need to talk with your client or teammate and closely examine how this decision will change things.

Most compromise issues are far less drastic than this, but the process for achieving a balanced situation is the same. Talk, exam-ine, and take some time to see how the changes will affect every-one involved. Getting the best terms possible is an appropriate business decision. However, if this is a new direction, you need your client to be willing to compromise and make the changes neces-sary so that both of you can feel comfortable and safe.

Compromise is an art form that successful leaders have be-come masters at. The key is understanding that you're not giving up or giving in—you're just seeking balance.

32 Kaizen

The journey of a thousand miles must begin with a single step.
—Chinese proverb

The Japanese philosophy of *kaizen* emphasizes that business gets better a little bit at a time. Progress is made in small, seemingly insignificant increments. This outlook can help any individual or company who wants to move forward. It is a tried-and-true way of thinking that can assist those who are dealing with almost any difficulty, including the current economic turmoil. It also can be very useful when reaching for a goal.

Dealing with a serious situation can be overwhelming. You may not know where to turn or what to do. Taking very small steps helps you to keep forging ahead and gives you a sense that you are doing something positive. That knowledge can make the difference between getting through your issues or suffering with them for a lifetime.

For a company or leader who is currently being beaten up by the economy, just getting into the office every day and facing the possibility of lay-offs or bringing your business back into the black may be monumentally challenging. Rather than focus on this entire task, you can instead take the small step of offering superior service and assistance to your current clients and team members. This is a great starting place. The next day you can start looking for new customers, and each day thereafter go a little further. These small steps add up quickly, and before you know it things will be back in balance—perhaps not as profitable as you would like, but under the circumstances, just staying afloat and keeping the doors open and your team paid is a huge success.

Most of the changes people make are not big ones. I usually suggest to clients that, instead of trying to make huge alterations in their lives, they find something small in their world to work on that first.

If you're not happy at work, look for one small thing that can make you feel better about what you do or whom you do it with. Perhaps taking a mental health day will get your head in the right place. Then you can start to make other small, progressive adjustments on a daily basis. You will be astonished at how quickly the changes add up and help you make positive and permanent shifts.

One of the better books on this subject is *The Kaizen Way* by UCLA professor Robert Maurer, Ph.D. One of the most poignant statements he makes is that "while the steps may be small, what we're reaching for is not." For those of us dealing with this huge transition, it's a reminder of how important it is to do something, even a very little something, each and every day to help you out of the pit or to achieve your dream.

With a little time and the goal of making very small improvements on a regular basis, you can create new business, reach your goals, and even make the world a better place. Give it a try. You'll be amazed at how quickly your team, company, and life will improve.

33

10 Reasons Why
We Don't Talk

*Don't hide your strategy under a bushel. Communicate it
throughout your company. It's better today to disclose
too much than too little.*
—Joel E. Ross

Communication is the greatest and perhaps least-used tool we
have to make our companies successful. Here are 10 reasons we
don't talk and how to make a correction when necessary.

1. Just because you disagree, doesn't mean you shouldn't talk.
In fact, that's exactly when getting into a deep conversation is
most important. Don't let your opinion stop communication
and impede progress. Talk about what you'd prefer and try to
find some balance and a way for you to get your points across.

2. Share your insights gently. If it's a difficult topic, to avoid
hurting a coworker's feelings and making him or her unproductive, or risk getting your boss mad at you, broach the subject as politely as possible. This will also help you resolve things
more easily.

3. It's hard to be part of the conversation if you feel like you're out of the loop. Remain informed on what's going on in the business world as well as your own company. That way you will always have something to contribute to the dialogue. Reading is your friend and will help you stay on top of what's going on.

4. Didn't I say that? Upon occasion, we believe we've had a conversation with our coworker when what actually happened is that we thought about the conversation instead of having it. Check with your teammate before you jump to the conclusion that you've already discussed the subject.

5. Some people are too lazy to want to engage in conversation. They'd rather hang around and stare out the window than use their energy to connect with coworkers or clients. If this is you or someone on your team, let her know what you see (remember tip 2) and ask if she needs some support or someone to talk to.

6. When your words are weary. There are times when even the best conversationalist will be too tired to put words together. Being too exhausted to talk is something you may experience at times. If this happens, tell your teammate that you need a break and you'd like to chat about this later. Make sure that you're the one who brings the topic up again.

7. Don't try to be a mind reader. You may think you know what your co-worker is going to say, and so you don't bother bringing it up. This type of behavior is a recipe for additional issues. Just say the words and avoid the problem.

8. Eavesdropping is an unreliable way to get information. Just because you think you've heard something doesn't mean you got it right. Check it our before you get offended or clam up.

9. Unhealed anger will cause almost anyone to withhold communication. If you're mad at someone you work with, tell him or her and get it out, so you can get back to normal. If someone is angry with you, tell him or her you're willing to talk about it. In this case, be the listener.

10. Take the time to talk with those you care for. Sometimes very busy people unconsciously forget to converse with those closest to them. Make sure that your life doesn't take away from your love. Check in on a regular basis. The conversations don't have to take long; they just have to take place.

The only way we have to really know what's going on around us is to talk with the people involved. Take every opportunity you have to communicate and connect with the people you work with and care about. The easiest way to do that is to talk with them.

Crisis Management

Step 4 will give you the foundation you need to deal with the current economy and any future crises that may happen. Planning is your best ally in confronting crisis, and it is amazingly helpful to train your team in critical incident management.

Given the global economy, chances are you will need to travel, and your business needs to be able to run without you when you are busy or away. Finding the tools to make this happen is part of this step. Some leaders and team members are addicted to work, and that creates its own set of problems. Learning to keep your cool while handling the inevitable crisis is what sets the best apart from the rest.

10 Tools to Plan for Crisis

If you don't know where you are going, you might wind up someplace else.
—Yogi Berra

How do successful executives plan for a crisis? Though each crisis may be different from the one before, they know that eventually another one is going to happen. They just don't know when. It's similar to having kids: crises don't come with a manual. Although most people just go with their guts and follow their instincts, some tried-and-true rules still apply.

Crisis management skills

Although every crisis is different, practicing executives who practice these skills usually get through the challenge more quickly and easily than those who don't.

1. Experience is the best teacher. There are two types of businesses: those that live through crisis and those that don't. The ones that continue to learn continue to live. That means, even

if the management team doesn't have all the answers from within, they seek it. They hire expertise. There are many seasoned consultants and even interim CEOs who are available to lead organizations through crises and challenges. There are even government organizations like SCORE (Service Core of Retired Executives) that help CEOs and other top executives. Alternatively, top management can continue to learn by joining a CEO or peer group, preferably before a crisis occurs. Participating in a mastermind group can save executives from reinventing the wheel and spinning yours as well.

2. Remain calm. Behavior is an extremely important tool. Do you clam up or get angry in a crisis? Because company personnel will reflect your behavior, executives who are distant or anxious create that same demeanor in their employees. It's tough leading under pressure. That's why it's advantageous to have an executive coach or even a therapist to lean on. If you're telling tales of woe to a bartender, it may be time to sell out.

3. Become idea prone. Some leaders get great ideas in a crisis. Do you? If you don't, engage in brainstorming tactics. Companies that use idea-generating techniques on a regular basis know the value of this practice. The more experience people have with creating ideas, the easier it will be to plan, avoid, or get out of trouble. If you are an Innovator, someone who is good at generating ideas, keep Implementers, those who are good at dealing with the details, close at hand and visa-versa. Ideas and the ability to carry them out are two different things.

4. Learn to communicate. It's the most important element in a crisis. Ninety percent of serious controversies result from misunderstanding. When situations become problematic, choose your words and messages carefully. They can help mitigate the challenges that arise. If perception dictates reality, the management person involved must be perceived as in control and as having the ability to use this crisis as a springboard. Some quick but effective communication tips include banning bad attitudes, conducting team-building activities,

and remaining available to the staff. Some executives think communication is a soft issue, but even the president of our country deals with it on a regular basis

5. Understand the grieving process. After a significant change, every company needs an adjustment period. Companies that don't make room for this psychological necessity find it more difficult to move ahead. Encourage and support your people to recognize and experience the loss, even if it's the loss that comes from giving up the "we've always done it this way" syndrome. Grief includes five key stages:

    1. Denial.

    2. Bargaining.

    3. Anger.

    4. Depression.

    5. Acceptance.

These may come in any order except for acceptance, which is always the final stage. Guide the team through the process, giving them room for their feelings to be expressed. Make sure to do the same for the leaders.

6. Find and express passion. It can make the difference between surviving and dying. It did for Holocaust survivors. It was their passion that allowed them to survive under the worst conditions imaginable. A company crisis cannot be nearly as bad; but the leaders passion has to be nearly as strong. Team members will look to their leader to guide them through the challenges ahead. If a leader momentarily loses their passion, they need to reach down to the depths of their souls and pull it up. It is their reason for being, their responsibility to their team and their drive to succeed. If leaders are unable to find it, they need to seek consultation. If they still can't find it—they need to find someone who can, and put them in charge.

7. Practice visualization. Good leaders hold their company's vision. Great leaders visualize their company's future. Imagine the power that could come when the entire team visualizes a successful outcome to its current crisis. That same power can

propel your business to the next level of excellence. Use this time to reinforce this incredible and underutilized tool. If it can cure cancer, it can change a business.

8.   Release your stress. Play golf; do yoga; run. Whatever it takes to release stress, do it. Don't keep frustration bottled up. Talk with someone about feelings and fears. As long as some steam is let off on a regular basis, pressure isn't a killer. Don't gloss over this point; as much as 80 percent of all terminal disease can be related to stress.

9.   Create a sound strategic plan. A good strategic plan has a contingency clause. The team that creates the plan will have discussed possible challenges, everything from a major market downturn, to a competitor stealing a large account, or even the phones going out. Look at as many possibilities as possible, run simulation exercises, and role-play a crisis. Team members will learn a lot about how they will react under pressure and about each other, as well as the strengths and weaknesses of the organization, during these exercises. In addition, this type of training is a great confidence builder.

10. Talk about what does and doesn't work. Having a trusted team member that you can run your concerns by is a great asset in the working world. It doesn't have to be a professional executive coach or a therapist (but don't avoid one if you need it). Someone with good listening skills may be all you need.

These tools are lifesavers in a crisis. They are the best practices of the most successful businesspeople on the planet. In graduate school they teach that, if ideas are taken from one source, it's plagiarism; if they are taken from many, it's research. There are very few problems that others haven't experienced. Learn from them, be prepared, and persist.

Leading in a Crisis

Crises refine life. In them you discover what you are.
—Allan K. Chalmers

This is an economic crisis, and things are different now. How this difference is manifested is yet to be seen. As with most things in life, what we are feeling and even fearing now will eventually change. Before it changes, however, there will be many different situations that will call upon every tool, tactic, tip, and trick we can muster. This is a crisis, and in crises, some tried-and-true emotional survival tools can be of help to you, your families, and your teams. Here are a few.

Become available

Be available to your teams. Sometimes just being around, just being visible, is enough. It gives someone the sense that they are not alone, and if trouble arises, help is nearby. In some circumstances, it's a bit like being a lifeguard. Most of the time we are just watching, but we need to always be ready to jump in if the need arises.

Being flexible and adaptable are core behaviors that have guided people through tragedy. We now know that circumstances can change at the drop of a hat, and not just for others, but for ourselves as well. If our relationships are a priority, as they should be, then changes can be adapted to and grown through. Being present is not counseling, but it does help people deal with unforeseen circumstances. You can help others through example, guidance, and presence.

Leadership listening skills

Mark Twain said, "We have two ears and one mouth because it's twice as hard to listen." Listening may be the most important part of your job right now. It may also be the most difficult. You can easily fall into the trap of someone that hears, but doesn't listen. The skill that needs to be developed can be called "listening with the third ear." This is where you listen for what is not being said; you listen for the feelings behind the words. This is where attention and intention, both good and bad, are obvious.

Many of us have complained in the past that we have had to be a therapist to our team members. Right now, the ability to listen and give understanding will help you and your people deal with the crisis at hand and the times ahead.

Understanding pressure

Pressure is a part of life. How we choose to react to it is really the challenge. Step one is to see it, step two is to acknowledge it, and step three is to do more than just talk about it. Doing this releases the steam from the pressure cooker and prevents an explosion, which usually causes a mess. Integrating this, and the other tools into your behaviors will keep you and your people emotionally healthy during these difficult days.

Pressure can be positive. It helps people feel alive and productive, and it makes life interesting. In fact, many of us thrive on pressure. On the other hand, it's stress that needs to be avoided, and stress happens when there is either too much or too little pressure in our lives. When you're in a situation like this, too much pressure can bring you to your knees. It can affect your health, your family, and your company.

Your internal pressure regulator

Sometimes it's difficult to recognize the pressure and stress of a tragedy, and the desire to do the right thing becomes overwhelming. It's the strongest of us that drive ourselves to distraction. Watch yourself, and listen to those closest to you. If you are advised that your tolerance level or work performance are suffering, take a serious look at your internal pressure regulator. You may be overdue for a break when you are short-tempered, depressed, or tired. We all have internal regulators that go off in different ways, but, if you are behaving in a manner that is not your norm or if you stop caring, it could be a warning signal from your internal pressure regulator.

Leadership and pressure

We are always dealing with some pressure. In good times, we seem to anticipate problems. In a time like this, we have not been able to conceive the crisis at hand. During the crisis, you will wear many hats—general, soldier, and therapist. Learning to let your people vent and training yourself to respond, not react, are important skills to master. Good leaders explain the challenge, and at the same time they share their vision for the future. They also look for the upside, while continually demonstrating their resolve. Because some crises can make or break an individual (not to mention a company or a country), it's important to find ways to release some of the pressure and maintain your role.

1-minute vacations

One of the most successful stress reduction techniques is the "1-minute vacation." It combines relaxation and visualization to create a psychological pressure release valve. To take this mini-vacation, simply visualize yourself in a beautiful and peaceful place. For example, your favorite might be a beach where you feel the relaxing, warm sun against your face, the wind in your hair, and the smell of the salt air. Next time the pressure builds, try this technique of picturing yourself in your peaceful place for 60 seconds. This little 1-minute vacation can release mounds of stress.

Rely on others

Nobody has all the answers. That's why it's important to get coaching and support from peers and friends. If you don't have the answers within, you need to seek them out. By seeking out the answers, you strengthen your own abilities. There are many seasoned counselors and groups that can offer support. You might even consider bringing a therapist into your company for a day. It could be of great help to your people, and, if nothing else, it is a powerful way of showing you care. Sometimes, that's all it takes, just showing in some way that you care.

Commit

Most crises are not nearly as bad as the national economic crisis we are currently in. To survive now, your commitment has to be strong. Team members will look to their leader to guide them through the challenges ahead.

Although this crisis is vastly more significant than most we have faced, people who practice these skills usually get through the challenge more quickly and easily than those who don't.

Pain in the Workplace

When written in Chinese, the word "crisis" is composed of
two characters—one represents danger, and
the other represents "opportunity."
—John F. Kennedy

We are in an economic downturn and still healing from a great national tragedy. Your business may be hurting and your team may be as well. Memorial Day, Independence Day, and regular air travel are poignant reminders that we are all doing business in a different world. The natural reaction is pain and fear, but this is business and we don't make room for emotions in business. The problem with that is, unless we allow ourselves and our teams to release the emotions, it is very difficult to move on and recreate our business and our lives. Emotions need to be processed so they can be released. If not, any situation that remotely resembles something hurtful or even worrisome can bring back the unhealed feelings. Emotions of this type can slow you and your business down, and make it difficult, if not impossible, to succeed.

It's a psychological fact that unreleased and unhealed emotions continue to affect us in a negative way. In business, we are used to dealing with the numbers and if they aren't good, then waiting for the next quarter to be better. We do our best to make our company look good, but neglect the importance of having a company that feels good. Ignoring feelings is a surefire way to end up in trouble. This isn't some touchy-feely excuse for a company sensitivity session, it's a hard-core fact.

When people are in fear or pain, they use most of their energy to deal with it. Their creative and implementation abilities are minimized because they cannot focus. Without processing, their feelings begin to run their life, and so the life of your company. Everyone feels what's going on, but no one communicates because this is business and there is zero tolerance for feelings. If we don't create a change in how this is currently handled we will not survive the current economic downturn or any crisis in the future.

The hard part isn't getting started; it's finding the willingness within yourself to allow it to happen. If you're concerned about entering into the process correctly, that is appropriate. Most leaders are not schooled in dealing with emotions, regardless of how much we think we do on a daily basis. Your best bet in this case is to bring in a professional. Your insurance may cover the cost, and a good counselor can be hired for as little as $100 per hour. Considering the value to your company and the devastating effects that fear and pain can have on your workforce, it's worth it—whatever the price.

Giving your people money or even time off isn't the answer. What they need, and may be unable to ask for, is help in dealing with their emotions. With the highest unemployment in the last generation, they may also be in fear of their jobs. If you have had recent lay-offs, this is a definite concern. They are talking about it around the water cooler and at home, so you'd better let them deal with it at work. If you choose to ignore it, their productivity will suffer and so will your bottom line.

Even if you haven't got a pressing issue that you can see, some kind of debriefing session, just to clear the air, will motivate your staff. This is the kind of support that builds lifelong loyalty in your workforce. Letting your people know that they are being supported emotionally as well as financially will help you create a winning team.

Encourage your people to talk about the pain they are feeling. If they are concerned with the economy (and who isn't), that may be a good place to start. Sharing feelings about the meltdown will lead them to releasing fear and pain about other work-related issues. If you have had a major downturn and had to resort to lay-offs, that's another good place to start. Just opening the door and letting the team know that you support them in this way will help your company prosper.

Critical Incident Training

Watch out for emergencies. They are your big chance.
—Fritz Reiner

People are losing their jobs and homes, crime is up, the term *going postal* has become a cliché, and elementary schools use metal detectors on a daily basis. Critical Incident Training (CIT) is now a must for companies that rely on their most valuable asset: their human capital. Although many organizations are re-emphasizing their safety procedures, such as evacuation plans and communication protocols, procedures to deal with the emotional effects of a tragedy need to be put in place as well. Companies need to help their people deal with the trauma in either a small group or, with the assistance of a licensed and professional psychotherapist, in an individual format. This is a service that is needed quickly and must be presented in a sensitive and skillful manner.

Who should seek CIT

A company's CIT program needs to be open to all employees, including supervisors, line employees, managers, service staff, and executives. This includes anyone who could benefit from a better understanding of their personal and professional ability to deal with a crisis. The class sizes should be limited to ensure maximum participation, and time also needs to be dedicated to dealing with any individual issues that may arise.

CIT workshops need to be designed to assist people in identifying how they feel about the tragedy. Their purpose is to help give a voice to company team member issues about a trauma or tragedy, while addressing classical and realistic solutions to their personal and professional questions. Everyone is feeling something about the recent economic crisis, and everyone wants to better understand what they and their co-workers are dealing with. People are also asking how they can be better prepared if things should get worse in the future.

Recognizing when trauma hits

The signs of trauma vary widely and may include people being distant, isolated, withdrawn, and avoiding thoughts, feelings, or conversations about the event. The signals of trauma may also manifest as frustrated, irrational, agitated, annoyed, or angry. Staff members may want retribution against other cultures or ethnic groups, even though they may have worked with them for years. Team members may also appear to be distracted, confused, or numbed by the situation.

Recurring or distressing dreams are a sign that some healing is needed. People who have lived through a trauma may have episodes of PTSD (post-traumatic stress disorder). Some individuals may use "gallows humor" or act in a nonsensical or immature fashion to compensate for their stress. When all else fails, denial is a powerful defense mechanism. Some people simply go into denial and refuse to believe that they/we are in a crisis, and those around them may find this behavior offensive.

Staff members need to become aware of recognizing their own triggers and behaviors as well of those of their coworkers. If companies want their people to maintain their previous productivity levels, they need to provide help for individuals and teams to talk about their emotions. The only ways to deal with the issues are to talk about them and create ways for individuals and teams to integrate new behaviors necessary for dealing with this most difficult situation.

Identifying anxiety and depression

The signs of anxiety include rapid heartbeat, clammy hands, nervousness, sweating, nausea, diarrhea, irritability, loss or increase of appetite, emotional instability, crying spells, sleep disorders, shaking, tremors, shortness of breath, feeling smothered, choking, or dizziness. If you notice these symptoms in yourself or in coworkers, take action sooner rather than later. Symptoms change shape and can become emotional killers if not dealt with.

The initial signs of depression can include symptoms such as feeling tearful, helpless, hopeless, withdrawn, irritable, agitated, or angry. Deeper symptoms can present as diminished interest or no pleasure in most activities, insomnia, hypersomnia (sleeping too much), fatigue or loss of energy, and feelings of worthlessness or inappropriate guilt. If the silent anguish of depression is allowed to continue, individuals may experience loss of focus or concentration, indecisiveness, significant weight loss or gain, recurrent thoughts of death, or even suicidal thoughts. Catching these symptoms in the early stages creates a much better prognosis for healing the problem.

Taking care of coworkers and yourself

The best way to help those around you is to let them have their feelings about this event; don't try to change or fix them. Let them talk about whatever they need to talk about. When they are talking, don't interrupt, interject, or interpret. Watching someone struggle with trauma is difficult and many of us naturally want to "fix" the problem. In the case of psychic wounds that occur with this kind of incident, trying to console or "band-aid" the person involved will only serve to lengthen the process. It is best to allow them the space to release any pent-up feelings.

Being a role model in this circumstance means taking care of yourself. Get back to your routines as soon as possible; be an example for others to follow. You also need to support others in getting professional help in the event that they may need it. If you choose to work with a professional therapist, be sure he or she has experience in dealing with trauma. Many people work with psychotherapists. More and more companies are bringing them in on a part-time basis, wheras others have them as full-time staff.

How to start "dealing with the feelings"

Some ways to help yourself and others include finding a person you can feel safe with and talk to about your feelings and what's going on with you. If that's too difficult right now, there are some effective alternative options including writing down your feelings in a journal. It is more effective to actually hand write, or print you words rather than type them into a computer. There is a different healing that takes place when pen hits paper.

That being said, some people would prefer going online and entering one of the myriad chat rooms that have appeared to help individuals deal with crisis. E-mails, texting, or instant messages with friends and family can also provide some needed support.

In order to begin

Start with an open discussion, interspersed with individual questions. Include practice exercises for stress reduction, and also detailed instruction on identifying symptoms. Provide participants with a documented account of their progress as well as a checklist for symptom identification and methods for continued improvement.

It is recommended that you use a professional to facilitate your CIT, but if you can't find a qualified person, or want to begin a CIT at your organization, the points previously mentioned will get you started.

Can Your Business Run Without You?

*No person will make a great business who wants to
do it all himself or get all the credit.*
—Andrew Carnegie

If you don't take vacations or start new projects because you're afraid of what might go wrong when you're not around, it's a symptom of a serious business dysfunction. You have ineffective-manageritis. If your direct reports cannot sit in your chair and do your job, you haven't trained them properly.

Think about it. If you have had to do damage control after taking some time away from the business, then some training of your key staff is in order. In the process, you can also ready your entire team to cope with a disaster, and these days that kind of planning is a necessity. You may have weathered the downturn so far, but what about the next crisis, and the next. Making sure that you have backup personnel is as important as having backup systems for your computers.

Yes, it will take some time, effort, and expense on your part to create an effective leadership program of this type. It is also helpful to understand that training is not a one-day off-site process, it is something that needs to be ongoing and always available.

In order to cover all the bases, I suggest that you work with a consultant or current team leader who has the integrity to understand that he or she can't be all things to all people and knows when to bring in other experts. Most trainers have a good network from which to serve their clients. If they don't, or they want to try to go beyond their scope of practice to keep your checks flowing to them, then change players.

As a leader, you need to be accountable for the continuous improvement of your company. The concept of accountability really needs to be ingrained within your entire management structure.

Here are some tips to help you get things going:

Encouraging Accountability

1. To get started, state your intentions and let your team know what you are going for.

2. Give your team members an article or put something in writing and make a date to discuss it.

3. Make an appointment with a consultant or trainer to brainstorm ideas. Most vendors will do it for free.

4. Have essential players join a mastermind group.

5. Ask the difficult questions with your team.

6. Create a shadow program, where new team members spend a day working with more seasoned staffers and learning what they do. This should take place at least once a month.

7. Do a company-wide evaluation.

8. Have teams set their own goals.

9. Let team members have input as to the type of training they want and need.

10. Follow-up. Follow-up. Follow-up.

Here's an example of why this process is so important. It is a well known fact that most people leave their jobs because they don't get along with their bosses. What this means is that you have to train leaders, managers, and supervisors to get along better with their team members. This is an interpersonal skill that requires brainstorming, consultation, and creativity.

Unfortunately, sending management leaders to a workplace psychology seminar is as effective as sending them to a movie. If there isn't any glue (coaching and accountability) to hold the knowledge together it won't stick. It's like going to a golf clinic for a weekend and then not playing the game for a month afterward you'll lose everything that you learned.

This is why continuing education through a professional who is accessible to your team members and who will customize what they deliver is so important.

Long-lasting professional development requires an emotional fitness mindset. Finding ways to educate your team to become more effective leaders will not only give you a break when you need it; it will also show up in your bottom line. This is the ultimate win-win scenario.

Are You a Workaholic?

It's true hard work never killed anybody, but I figure,
why take the chance?
—Ronald Reagan

If you are more comfortable at work than in any other environment, or if you feel as if you can't take a vacation, or don't have the ability to just turn off work for a few days, you may actually be a workaholic.

Whether it's addiction, avoidance, or an obsessive-compulsive disorder, workaholism is harmful to its victims and those who are close enough to feel the fallout. Additional signs can include using work as an escape, having your home become a "satellite office," and being unable to be at peace when you're not thinking about or doing work. An inability to relax or to enjoy your free time is another signal that you could be in the process of becoming, as John Bradshaw once said, "A human-doing rather than a human-being."

Hard work and achievement are good things, but if they take the place of loved ones or even taking care of yourself, you need to

149

take a deeper look at what's driving you. This includes using work to avoid personal or family issues.

For some, living to work may actually mean working to live. When struggling to make ends meet, working overtime at every opportunity is totally understandable. These are difficult situations, but to maintain good health, you need to build in some downtime. The difference between needing to work and workaholism lies in whether or not you can stop thinking about your job when you are away from it.

Others who overwork may have a severe need to be perfect and feel that no one else can do the job as well as they can. Sometimes a workaholic may fear losing a job, so he or she puts in the extra effort to insure job security.

There are occasions when overwork can be beneficial. If you are healing from an emotional wound, trying to build a nest egg, or fighting bad habits, concentrating on work can be a good idea. Just make sure that you keep some balance in your life.

Workaholics Anonymous has a Website (*www.workaholics-anonymous.org*) where you can take a test, get some basic information about support groups, and learn about some things you can do to dial your work life back a little bit.

A couple of good tips for dealing with this issue include taking long weekends and vowing during time off not to tackle any work-related projects. Another tip is to make your personal time a sacred space where you can only do things for yourself or your loved ones.

As issues go, this may not be perceived as the worst thing in the world. But I have seen it ruin numerous companies and relationships, both professional and personal. I have also met many very successful people who felt alone in the world because so much of their time was spent at their businesses instead of with those they love.

Culturally, we tend to honor hard work, and most people feel that it pays off. But in the end, if it replaces the more important things in life, like relationships, you end up with less.

Failures Are Stepping-Stones to Success

Emotions have taught mankind to reason.
—Marquis De Vauvenargues

With the humblest of apologies to Sir Charles Darwin, I don't believe that survival of the fittest applies any longer. I think that in the world today, knowing how to handle failures, and also how to use them to move ahead, is what will determine which companies go the way of the Dodo bird and which evolve.

If you were to ask those who have made their lives meaningful, I am sure that the vast majority would say that their failures taught them lessons and gave them the inspiration to succeed. I know whenever I am asked how I got here (wherever that is), I say that it was by making a lot of mistakes and learning from them.

Turning a perceived failure into a stepping-stone isn't rocket science; it's one part inspiration and two parts perspiration. For example, as a writer I get rejected on a regular basis (which kinda reminds me of finding a date for the prom). I read what editors say, get exasperated, complain needlessly, make some useless phone calls, send some even more useless e-mails, and think heavily about becoming the lawyer my mother wanted.

After I've exhausted myself purging the initial disappointment, I finally look at what was said and begin making the necessary changes in the manuscript.

It may take you some time and practice to develop your own process, but there is no question that you and whatever you are working on, be it personal or professional, will be better for it.

This kind of thinking also improves your problem-solving skills so that, the next time you have a challenge, you'll have more ideas and energy to correct the situation. It also builds your confidence, because you fixed the problem yourself. Those who take the easy way out, and simply walk away from a possible failure, never reap those benefits. They also spend the rest of their lives wondering what could have been, and for me that's a very sad prospect.

To begin the stepping-stone approach, start by believing that you haven't failed; you just found some ways that didn't work for you at the moment. Your work might need to be tuned up, but don't scrap it. Keeping a file of all your ideas, the ones that worked and the ones that didn't, is a great way to avoid losing a good idea. Even if it wasn't the right one the first time you thought of it, you may well find a use for it in the future.

There is an old saying that those who do not learn from their mistakes will repeat them. A wise person is someone who learns from failures. It may not feel like a good thing when you first discover that you've made an error, but we all know it's human. Using those missteps to help you reach the next level—now that's divine.

Problems at Work

The best way to escape from a problem is to solve it.
—Alan Saporta

Sometimes, it seems that our business life can be best described as learning how to get from one problem to the next as gracefully as possible. For most of us still standing on planet Earth, every day produces a variety of challenges. It's not how you look at it or what your attitude is; it's actually more about accepting that work, like life, is never going to be perfect.

The drive for perfection is not a bad thing. But when something throws you off and causes you to shut down and blow a deal or walk off the field in a huff when your team doesn't win, it's a sign that your priorities may be out of order.

Some people are great at helping us solve our problems. Our trusted team members, as well as numerous consultants, can give amazing advice, but those same people may hit a wall when it comes to dealing with their own issues. No matter what someone else tells us, the resolution of any dilemma still rests on our shoulders.

Sometimes our problems can best be solved by the passage of time. This does not mean you should ignore your clients or your bills. It means that a night, or even a few days, can actually make a big difference in what you choose to do.

If you can't resolve the problem by sleeping on it, try writing down your feelings about the issue. You can also list the pros, cons, and alternatives. These tried-and-true techniques actually help you release uncomfortable feelings by getting them out of your head and onto the paper. This gives your mind some extra space to look at things differently.

Viewing a problem from another perspective is also a very productive technique. Asking yourself "how would someone I respect (Bill Gates, for example) deal with this?" can help you to see things differently. Imagine the person in your head and listen to what he or she would say.

When your worklife seems to be dominated by difficulty, it's also important to refrain from negatively judging yourself. It's easy to blame or be shamed, and the truth is that sometimes, no matter how well you plan, things go wrong. Taking difficulty in stride is much easier when you see it as a part of normal business life.

Dealing with the emotional aspects of an issue can be hard. If your feelings are causing you to obsess or be anxious, try diverting your attention. Almost any activity will do. If you're keyed up take a walk; if you're tired, take a nap. Your brain will work better when you let go of the stress.

Whatever your issue, these tools can make it easier, but perhaps the best advice is to remember that a company or a position without problems doesn't exist or isn't evolving.

42

10 Tools for
Keeping Your Cool

*Nothing gives one person so much advantage over another
as to remain cool and unruffled under all circumstances.*
—Thomas Jefferson

Keeping your wits about you when the staff is acting up, your boss is down on you, and the economy is all over the map can be a challenge. Here are 10 tools to help you manage your mood and maintain your balance.

1. Think before you act. This includes saying things as well as doing them. Putting your brain in gear before engaging in a verbal assault will help you prevent any escalation and keep the situation under control.

2. If someone hurts you, let him or her know it. Don't hold it in or act it out. Simply say, "What you said hurt my feelings. Please don't do that again." I know it hasn't been the way business is done, but it needs to be so it might as well start with you.

3. Learn about your triggers and avoid them. For example, if traffic drives you crazy, take the scenic route. If someone at work constantly asks unsuitable questions and makes you

insane, gently tell him or her to dial it back. If that doesn't work you may need to send a note to a supervisor. It may take a little inventiveness, but eliminating the stress is worth it.

4.   The old counting-to-10 trick works. If you've never tried it, I suggest you give it a shot. The next time something or someone frosts your cookies, just slowly count, and with each number remind yourself that by getting upset you are only hurting yourself.

5.   Pretend you're above it all. When the limo driver is late, or you have to go through security before your private jet takes off, keep it in perspective. After all, you have a great life, and these minor inconveniences are just a part of the real world that we all have to live in.

6.   Don't sweat the small stuff. Birth and death are the only two biggies in life. Everything else is not worth getting your knickers in a twist. Learning to let go will help you to live longer.

7.   Take a few deep breaths. It's amazing how many people hold their breath when they get upset. Forcing fresh air into your lungs sends oxygen to your heart and brain and acts as a calming agent. Breathe slowly and be sure not to hyperventilate. If you get really upset, breathe into a paper bag.

8.   Check in with your heart. Asking yourself if this is truly where you want to be, and how you want to feel or act toward another person (or in front of strangers), can be a great reminder to hold your tongue.

9.   Think before you speak. Saying to yourself what you might say to another, and imagining how he or she will take it, is a great way to prevent downward spirals from occurring.

10. Ask yourself, "Am I a positive person or a negative person?" This question has inspired many people (adults and children) to keep their attitudes in check. Keeping a positive attitude is not just a cliché, it makes your world a better place to be.

When the waters of business are rough, you need to keep your wits about you, so you can navigate what's coming. If you don't keep your ship steady, you may just end up like the Poseidon—upside down.

Mentoring and Motivating

Step 5 will teach leaders and managers how to inspire their team members and create solid mentoring programs. In addition, it shows everyone involved how to encourage one another and create a culture of mentoring. This is where your team learns, develops, and shares ideas that will make the individuals and the company better. Cost-free tools such as appropriate recognition and learning opportunities will help you build a top-flight team that will work together with mutual respect.

10 Tips for Motivating Your Team

There is only one way to get anybody to do anything.
And that is by making the other person want to do it.
—Dale Carnegie

Motivating a team is as much of an art form as it is alchemy. You must combine the power of emotion with the desire of your workforce. Once you do anything is possible. Here are 10 tools to help you do just that.

1. Lead with passion. If you are a low energy leader, your team and company will reflect your energy. This will not get the job done. Your passion is everything. Without it, success will elude you. Whatever you have to do to reclaim your excitement do it. Without being 100-percent into what you're doing, and sharing the commitment with passion, you won't be able to reach your goals.

2. Share your vision. Propose it, print it, and post it. Let everyone see it every day. It helps your people stay the course and reminds them of a higher purpose. If you don't have a vision

159

statement as of yet, get your top people together, order in lunch, and create one. Do it now.

3. Understand your purpose. If making money is your only purpose, you may achieve it, but the resulting experience will be empty. Helping your team grow, as people and in their careers, gives you a much higher purpose and will inspire you and them.

4. Educate and enlighten your team. The more people know, the better job they will do. In addition, offering them some education builds loyalty. Many companies pay for MBA programs with powerful results. Also, try the Knowledge Lunch idea; bring in an outside professional to teach industry insights once a week.

5. Treat team members like volunteers. This may be a difficult concept to grasp, after all, we do pay them. The idea here is to make them feel that their presence and contributions are valued. People give their all when they feel valued.

6. Be present and available. Do you have an MBWA? That's Management by Walking Around. Your team needs to know that their head coach is there if the going gets tough. Most of the time, just knowing that there is someone to turn to gives people the strength to figure out problems for themselves first.

7. Keep it together. Don't rage at anyone in front of your team. (Actually you shouldn't have to do that at all.) Don't criticize someone in front of another. (It could get you sued.) Treat yourself and your people with this respect and they will honor you and your company in the same manner.

8. Reward attempts. If you only reward success, your people will not be inspired to try harder. Let them know that failure is part of the success process and reward them for trying. It gives them the inspiration to invent and create—remember Post-Its.

9. Celebrate success. Most of the time after a success we say, "What's next?" Take some time, outside of work, to celebrate with those that are helping you to succeed. Also remember to pat yourself on the back from time to time.

10. Ask for their opinion. In addition to money, what keeps them at their job? What do they think the company needs to do to succeed? What have they learned from working there? These are the type of questions that, when asked, will make them feel that they are valued, and will also give you insight into how to improve your business.

Getting your team motivated requires that you truly believe in them and what you are doing. In this case they will feel it if you're not really on board.

Creating a Company Mentoring Program

One does not become a guru by accident.
—James Fenton

Do you now have or have you ever had a mentor? Those of us who have been fortunate in that area have a received a priceless gift. If you have experienced the professional and personal growth that comes from a great mentoring relationship then you will understand the value that comes from creating your own company mentoring program (CMP). On the other hand, if you have not yet lived this experience, keep reading—perhaps the following will inspire you.

A mentor's job is to help us maximize our potential and our performance. The good ones see things in us that we are not able to see ourselves. Had my mentors not told me I could, and helped me believe in myself and supported me in taking risks, I would not be successful.

If your company team believed that they could, and were supported to create more and better business, wouldn't you be more

163

successful? A company mentoring program will greatly assist you in achieving that goal.

The basic premise is elegantly simple; everyone in the company has some type of a mentor. The person who has been there one day can be mentored by the person who has been there two days. The CFO can be mentored by a board member and the CEO by the chairman. The objective is to have everyone in the company supported by someone who shares the goal of helping the mentee maximize his or her potential. This will bring value to your team and your clients, and help you grow your people.

10 Steps to Creating a Company Mentoring Program

1. Decide that creating a CMP is right for you and your company.
2. Start by getting buy-in from your team and being the first to mentor someone.
3. Ask for opinions about what your team wants in a CMP; find out what your people need to be top-level performers.
4. Begin with just a few people, but all at different levels in the company, so the results will be seen by everyone.
5. Get a mentor for yourself.
6. Create a culture by being open about your own mentor/mentee relationships.
7. Build trust with those participating. Listen to their experiences and ideas.
8. Spotlight mentor/mentee relationships. If you have a company newsletter, let each team share something they learned from each other.
9. As team members see results, they will ask for mentors, and that is the time to begin your company wide program.
10. Get your team-wide recognitio. Share the results with everyone (including clients) you can.

Creating a good CMP or even an individual mentoring relationship is a process, and it takes time. If you integrate just one of the steps on page 164 every month, you will be doing well and will have a program in place in less than a year.

It has been said that we learn best by teaching and teach best what we most need to learn. In that light, we become better mentors by being mentored. Look at who was a great mentor in your life. What was it that made him or her great? Understanding this will give you a good foundation to mentor, and remind you of how important your mentors have been to you.

Behaviors of Successful Mentors

*My chief want in life is someone who shall
make me do what I can.*
—Ralph Waldo Emerson

Great mentoring is not easy. There are many sacrifices and challenges along the way. Those who have succeeded did so by integrating certain behaviors into their skill sets. These behaviors made them better mentors, better leaders, and better people.

To get better at mentoring, or anything else for that matter, we must learn to endure feedback. This allows us to achieve growth. Taking conflict, controversy, and criticism in stride is not natural; it is a learned behavior. It requires careful examination of your feelings during and after any difficult situation or communication. Look at your own defensiveness, it can manifest in a number of ways, such as anger, sadness, denial (I never do denial, but some people do), even fear. If you can understand and get past your defensiveness, then learning can take place. Realizing that your position comes with difficult circumstances is a powerful step in moving from manager to mentor.

Successful mentors reject failure, limiting language and negative thinking. They never see failure as an ending; instead, they view it as a stepping-stone. They also strive to teach managers to avoid limiting language and negative thinking. One of Henry Ford's famous quotes is "Whether you think you can or think you can't, you're right!" He would not allow his team to say or think "can't" and mentored them to innovate when they encountered a road block. This rejection of negativity and failure allowed him to build an empire. How far could you and your team go if you eliminated the idea of failure?

Chemistry and connection

Creating the right chemistry is an integral piece of the mentor/mentee relationship. This connection between mentor and mentee cannot be assigned; it has to grow and develop. If you have assigned a mentor to someone, and the two do not have good chemistry, don't try to fix it. Much time and feelings will be saved if you simply pair them up with other people. Even with the best intentions, unbalanced chemistry will only result in an explosive relationship.

A mentor's job is to create a connection with her protégé, to help him do his best, and to hold him accountable. We chose our mentors because we admired their successes, or they were chosen for us because our behaviors and goals were aligned. Understand that our mentors will never comprehend the whys and wherefores of our behaviors. They are not there to be therapists. This relationship is not about probing someone's psyche; it is about helping people grow.

The mentor's gift

"My mentor is always there for me," says Michael Blumenthal of General Dynamics AIS Department. "It is one of the reasons our relationship really works; I know I can count on him." To succeed, mentors have to be available to their protégés. It gives them the sense that they are not alone and that if there is a question, help is nearby.

Being flexible and adaptable are core behaviors of successful mentors. Wise and experienced mentors know that circumstances can change at the drop of a hat, and not just for their protégé but for themselves as well. If the relationship is a priority, as it should be, then changes can be adapted to and grown through. Mentors help us deal with unforeseen circumstances, and the good ones are able to bend when necessary. They help us do the same through example, guidance, and presence.

The big picture here is to align your behavior with your values. It's your behaviors that teach your protégé. What you do and how you do it speaks louder than anything you could say.

Mentoring is NOT Therapy

The speed of the boss is the speed of the team.
—Lee Iacocca

Have you ever had to deal with a team member's emotional or personal problems? It's normal for a mentor/manager to spend time dealing with his or her coworker's problems, but when those problems become emotional, you may feel (rightfully so) that you really don't want to deal with these kinds of issues. You may also feel that you are out of your league. If a staff member's problems made you feel uncomfortable, it's a sign that you need to refer them to, or bring in, a professional counselor.

Counseling is NOT in your job description

It is not your job to be a therapist to your team members. Spending your time dealing with people problems has its limits. Although we have all had to deal with unexpected emotions like tears, silence, or outright anger, it really should not be part of your duties. What is in the mentors/manager's job description is having the ability and insight to know when to leave it to the pros.

Because mentoring is becoming a large part of our contemporary business culture, many consultants have added executive coaching to their repertoire. In addition, numerous psychotherapists (most with no business experience) have also become "executive coaches." Where mentoring and coaching are similar to each other, counseling is a completely different line of work. It involves dealing with people's emotions and helping to heal their neurosis. Just because someone calls himself or herself a coach, does not mean that they have the ability to counsel. Before you refer someone to counseling, make sure that the person they see has some training in psychology.

A mentor's job

Being a mentor means setting an example, listening to your team members, discussing their issues, and giving them leadership. Sometimes this means challenging them. A trained counselor understands that if you challenge people who are emotionally vulnerable or unstable, they may break down right in front of you, and they are prepared and educated for that. In addition, they are cautious about challenging someone who is very angry or unable to articulate his or her thoughts. This is a possible sign of instability, and could lead to the person could acting out or even "going postal." This is why it's so important to understand the risks of counseling, and why a mentor needs to stay within certain boundaries.

If someone comes to his mentor with a work-related issue, which may involve communication problems with a coworker, it falls under a mentor/manager's job description to help him resolve the issue. If a staff member is asking for help with a domestic issue, a substance abuse problem, or controlling his anger, he should be referred to a counselor, or to your company's EAP (employee assistance program), if you have one, or to a licensed mental health professional if you don't.

If a mentor or manager tries to deal with highly charged emotional issues, she could be putting themselves and the company at risk. They could also give inappropriate advice to the staff member and cause her personal harm.

Determining the objectives

When team members come to you with an issue that you think may cross the personal/professional line, you must first determine their goal in bringing the issue to you. Do they just want to unload—to have someone listen to them? Do they need your help is dealing with a coworker? Are they looking for advice or in need of counseling? Asking them directly what their objectives are can save both of you time and energy, not to mention grief.

Once you (and they) understand their needs, you can decide if this is an issue you are comfortable dealing with. If you are not comfortable, you need to be honest and direct them to someone who can help them deal with the issue. Don't just ignore it; it's part of your responsibility as a mentor to help them locate assistance.

Responsibility and benefits

Be careful not to fall into the Father/Mother confessor trap. Sometimes it is tempting to want to be the all-knowing mentor and take on problems that you don't have the training to deal with. Mentors like to be helpful; it's part of what motivates them to take on the role. Sometimes mentors don't want to admit that they may be in over their heads, and will continue to try to help a staff member without realizing they haven't got the skills. This isn't helpful to anyone, and it can result in actually making the problem worse and killing the mentor/mentee relationship.

Mentors have a responsibility to the people who come to them for guidance. This responsibility is one of the benefits of being a mentor; it makes mentors better leaders. Understanding boundaries and limitations gives mentors a greater ability to help others. It also allows them to grow personally and professionally.

Tactics of Great Mentors

*People are changed, not by coercion or
intimidation, but by example.*
—Anonymous

Could you use some great tactics to help motivate and grow
your team? Understanding a tactical approach is your first step.
Unlike strategic plans, tactics are processes you can immediately
put to use. The key is not just implementing these ideas, but doing
it in such a way as to achieve positive results in the short term. Here
are some tactics used by great mentors in some very successful
companies.

The truth about motivation

Motivation is a word that has been kicked around in business
for more than 50 years. The trouble is that we keep coming up with
superficial "incentives" that can make team members feel insulted
or cheapened. Nothing that you can give a person (short of a yacht)
will motivate them as much as recognition and support from their
supervisors and peers.

Tactics like "Employee of the Month" don't work because you only create one winner—and dozens of losers. The philosophy that "when one of us wins, we all win," creates a team out of a staff. That is the definition of *esprit de corps*.

As companies merge or acquire, the team members can suffer. A good mentor/manager believes in publicly recognizing the contributions of their entire team by celebrating large and small successes, and making the effort to mentor team members into positions that require them to become leaders.

If the team members know their mentors and managers support them, they have the gumption to take risks, to try new ideas and experiment. These are the behaviors that help companies grow. Support and recognition are the most powerful motivation tools a mentor can use. Encourage your people to step up to the plate, recognize them for making the effort, and reward them substantially when they hit a home run.

Pay for performance

Merit raises, giving a salary increase because someone has been with the company for a period of time, are not an effective tactic. Unfortunately, most people won't do any more than they have to, unless you give them a reason. Rewarding performance, large and small, is highly effective and results in a better bottom line for the company and the team member. This tactic has been used by sales teams for decades and is now finding its way into mainstream business.

The "pay for performance" practice leads to stronger teams because individuals realize that they depend on their teammates to create business. A natural mentoring process takes place when a sales closer works with a lead generator to insure proper prospecting. Some closers "spiff" (small cash or equivalent rewards) their lead generators for successive prospecting. Likewise a sales manager will "spiff" those who close a certain amount of sales. These are small examples of performance rewards, but there is a bigger picture.

Everyone wants to be part of something larger than they are, like a growing company. Tactics such as an ESOP or Phantom Stock/

Equity have proven to be highly effective motivation tools. In addition, mentoring your team to reach goals by significantly rewarding them creates profound results.

Self-evaluations

People know how well they are doing, and what they are not doing well. Most of the time mentors are more concerned with telling their charges how to do better rather than asking them what they think they are doing right. In an honest relationship, both parties should be able to express their feelings about their progress. If team members truly want to grow, they will be able to have objectivity about their performance.

There are several evaluation questions that can help create a positive dialogue and make the self-evaluation process more effective than a typical performance review. (See Chapter 6.) These questions will be great fuel for helping you both understand how progress is being made and what course corrections are necessary. It also opens the door for some serious career mentoring. Most importantly, it will help you both discover the skills that need to be developed in order to achieve your mutual goals.

Don't take away their problems

When things get hectic and scary, as they are now, and a team member comes to you with a problem that you can clearly see the answer to, it is tempting to solve it for him or her. This is not mentoring. By solving others' problems, you take away their opportunity to become educated, and their ability to solve problems for themselves. People learn best when they face new challenges, and in addition they gain the skills to solve other, more difficult problems. Ask them to first think about the issue and create a document about their problem and how they would best solve it. Taking the time to write about it helps the solutions become clear. Go over the options together, and you will both begin to create a new system and skill set for the majority of your teams problem-solving issues.

Using the tactics tactfully

Understanding and utilizing this tactic, and those mentioned previously, will help you mentor your team members to become more effective and to become leaders and mentors themselves. These are the tactics that will make your mentoring process an exciting part of your company culture. In addition, your team members will be inspired to reach new levels of performance; this is the essence of mentoring.

Recognition:
the Power of the Pen

*I have yet to find the man, however exalted his station,
who did not do better work and put forth greater effort
under a spirit of approval than under a spirit of criticism.*
—Charles M. Schwab

Olympic gold medals. The Oscars. The Emmys. A Nobel Peace Prize. The Stanley Cup. The Kennedy Center Lifetime Achievement Awards. The closest most of us get to any one of these honors is to watch the ceremonies through a television screen. We see the recipients radiate, sometimes with tears streaming down their faces while they thank all those who supported them in realizing their dream. The emotion chokes us. The elation lifts us. For a moment we soar along with them. We can imagine those feelings of acknowledgment, of being seen, of being heard, of knowing that our life's work has been recognized.

We then turn the television off, and it's back to "the real world." In the business environment, I have witnessed people being absolutely oblivious to thanking others for the magnificent jobs they do day in and day out. It is simply astounding. What's even more astonishing to me is that not only do most leaders forget to recognize others, but they don't even recognize themselves and the contributions they make to their own company.

Somehow in this society we have confused fame with recognition. The sad by-product is that only the famous are recognized. I don't believe that only the stars deserve to be honored. What about the company heroes you encounter on an everyday basis?

How about the HR manager who juggles 150 personalities, not to mention the reams of paperwork attached to that many employees? What about the PR team who makes your company shine in numerous press releases, brochures, and even the national press? Or the IT department who literally knock themselves out figuring out and fixing a software problem, one that could fold your company, but one that will never even be a concern for you because those everyday wizards take care of it "all in a day's work"?

As human beings, and as professionals, we need to be recognized. In a world where there is so much media and global overload, it's all too common for most people to go unrewarded. Any psychologist can tell you that, for most humans, recognition is more important than money and is the number one motivator of your people.

The people you work with need to know that they are valued. That goes beyond the standard paycheck at the end of the week. Think about it; when it comes down to it, as an employer you simply rent your team members' time—you don't own them. Renting time may not sound like such a big deal until you realize it is the single most precious commodity in the world—our time on earth. I really believe recognition, appreciation, and reward are crucial to survival in the marketplace today. It's simply good business.

I had a passionate, almost heated debate with a CEO during a business lunch on this very subject. His stance was, if you praise people, they will go soft on you. They will know they are doing well and will not work as intensely as if you consistently kept them "on the edge" wondering if they mattered. His company went from $150,000,000 to zero within a year because his team abandoned him for better environments, and they took their clients with them.

A simple pat on the back, a mention of thanks, can literally move mountains in the working world. In my experience most people are hard-working and capable, and take pride in the work they do. Loyalty has to be earned, and to earn it you have to acknowledge a job well done. Productivity rises for teams that are rewarded for the work they do. It's a simple fact. Your bottom line rises with a team that feels appreciated.

A great and free idea is a handwritten thank you note on company letterhead. (It should be a glowing statement.) A small note of thanks left on someone's desk or in his or her mailbox can lift a team member in ways you may never imagine. This is perhaps one of the most valuable ways to reward a great employee. An addition to this great tactic is to hand him or her the note and shake his or her hand in front of the rest of the team, stating your gratitude for a job well done.

These personal moments add up and create loyalty, and team members who will go above and beyond as well as creating a work environment that will encourage your team members to hang in through the inevitable rough times. It also has the added benefit of helping to attract good people and keeping them.

So unleash that expensive fountain pen you got for the holidays and write a couple of thank-you cards. Once you see the effect, I am sure you'll make it a regular activity.

Refining Your Mentoring Skills

*A pat on the back is only a few vertebrae removed from
a kick in the pants, but is miles ahead in results.*
—Ella Wheeler Wilcox

Mentoring is a process. It doesn't happen all at once. There are a number of tools that many successful mentors and mentoring programs use to create positive results and maximize the productivity of their organizations. These are tools you can teach to your management teams, who can then in turn utilize and teach these tools to their teams.

Promoting participation

People that participate in your company mentoring program (CMP) should be recognized and rewarded, although most will say that their mentoring relationship is enough of a reward. Have mentor/mentee meetings or events, but let everyone in the company attend. Encourage those who have begun this practice to talk to others in the company. This helps spread the word to those who may not yet be comfortable with the idea. Find as many ways as you can to promote participation in your CMP. In most companies that have developed successful programs, everyone (including the CEO) is assigned a mentor. At Accenture, for example, every team member has two mentors: a formal mentor, who helps guide their long term (strategic) career goals, and a project mentor, who helps them deal with short term (tactical) goals. It has become a very important part of their company culture and has helped make Accenture a very successful company.

In the spirit of promoting participation, it's best if everyone in the company participates, so the internal PR has to be good. Help your team see the value in having and being a mentor, make it part of your company culture. Be tough on holdouts, but remember, you can't mandate successful relationships, you have to build them.

Failure is part of the process

A good mentor allows for failure. A great mentor pursues it. If people are not failing, they are not making enough attempts. In order to grow, we must pursue failure; it's a necessary part of the path to success. It is the mentors' job to not just allow for failures, but to help their protégé learn from them. Sam Walton was a strong believer in pursuing failure. When something didn't go right, he would try a different way or take on a new challenge immediately.

Contemporary training

How much does it cost to locate, hire, train, and integrate a new person into your company? Training is one of the best ways to help your team grow and learn. It is also much more cost effective than finding new people. Think about growing your own experts. Investing in someone's education is a wise business move, and it builds loyalty on both sides. A mentoring relationship is about growth; offering or finding training for your proteges is one of your primary functions. Become aware of their needs and of what training is available and appropriate. Start with the tried and true, and then help them grow by encouraging them to take risks and try the new and unusual.

Choose wisely

To create a CMP in your company, you must pick your issues and tools carefully. Those listed above are used by the best mentors to help their people maximize their performance and help their businesses grow. Consider where you need to grow your company and you will better understand how to grow your people. Creating a CMP will help you get to the next level, whatever it is. Choose one idea per month to integrate into your company. In a very short time, mentoring will become part of your culture and your team will be making achievements you may not have dreamed possible.

Reward innovation

If we fall short of a goal, it is not a failure. The only failure is in not trying to achieve your vision. Wise mentors teach their teams to innovate. Look at how far you've gottten, realize what you have learned, and then see where you can go from here. If a goal is not achieved on a first, or even second, try, it means that more learning, brainstorming, and perhaps even a reshuffling of the players are necessary. Successful leaders celebrate their people attempting new ideas, rather than prohibiting them from trying or inducing a fear of failure.

Unannounced celebrations are a great way to acknowledge your team's attempts and to keep your morale and your team emotion high. When things are tough, good mentors utilize positive emotional reinforcement. Simply put, don't beat them when they are down—lift them up. Throw your team a low-end party or give them a small gift just because they tried (cut loose with some of those polo shirts you've been saving). Showing your respect for their efforts, especially in the face of adversity, is a very powerful mentoring and motivational tool.

Rewarding innovation is a great way to inspire your team to create new ideas and to try new methods. Good mentors reward inventiveness because it motivates their team to continue trying new ways to make things better. Several companies have gone as far as to create an "Innovation of the Year" award, with a trip and time off as the grand prize. If your team knows that there is a pot of gold at the end of the rainbow, they will be motivated to find it. As a mentor you are in the position to support your team to innovate, we all find it easier to try new things when we know we have a strong person beside us.

Cost-free mentoring and motivation

Probably the least expensive and most effective is the highly unutilized "thank you." Just shaking someone's hand (preferably in the company of their peers and supervisor) and saying something like, "I'm very glad you are working with us. Thank you." This will take someone's self-esteem to the next level. Acknowledging someone every chance you get is an opportunity to make your company more productive.

Saying "thanks" is a way of showing your emotions, and emotions are a constant in your business. One of the ways we keep clients is through their emotional connection to our company, products, or services. The same holds true for our team members; it is their emotional connection to their company that motivates or demotivates them. If their mentor and their company leaders show their emotions, the fear of a hidden agenda reduces, and people are much more willing to share their feelings about ideas, company progress, and their coworkers. If there are problems, you need to know about them as soon as they occur. Having an environment of openness creates the opportunity for people to be honest with difficulties instead of hiding them until it's too late.

Let them know you care

Good mentors are role models; they lead by example and maintain their integrity. They show that they care because no one cares how much you know, until they know how much you care. Mentoring can only work in an environment that promotes caring. It may sound touchy-feely, but, until we learn to understand to the emotions of the people on our teams, we can't understand how to inspire them. If your team members feel cared about, they will care about your company.

Great expectations

A good mentor does not accept mediocre performance. It is part or a mentor's duty to set and maintain high expectations. If you do not, your protégé will not rise to that level. It is natural and normal to stay with what is familiar and comfortable. Great mentors keep their mentees on the edge and acknowledge their successes while keeping their eyes on the summit of achievement. Goal-setting has become a cliché; we sometimes forget where it's real power lies.

The Magic of
Mastermind Groups

A great person is one who affects the mind of their generation.
—Benjamin Disraeli

Have you ever wondered how successful businesspeople became great leaders and captains of industry? My research on how the greats in business, the arts, politics, and life got there revealed that they had one thing in common. They were all members of some type of mastermind group.

Where do leaders go to deal with problems that only present themselves to the top dog? The old saying "it's lonely at the top" can be resolved appropriately in a top-flight mastermind group, where there are other people who understand what it's like to be in your position to talk with.

Did you know that Thomas Edison, Alexander Graham Bell, Henry Ford, and Harvey Firestone were all members of a mastermind group? This group of leaders knew something many of us do not. They knew they couldn't create in a vacuum, and relied on each other for feedback, ideas, and accountability. They met several times a year and were the closest of friends. They called themselves the Wayfarers. They also controlled much of the industry in our country for many years.

In a business framework, a mastermind group acts as an informal board of directors/advisors. Most are composed of CEOs, business owners, and executives from 12 to 15 non-competing businesses. The reason the members are non-competing is simple: the participants want to be able to share sensitive information in a safe and secure environment where everything is confidential. Occasionally, members do business with each other, but it is best to keep business out of the group in case something occurs that could damage the relationship between participants. This way the members are able to share ideas, ventures, and both personal and professional issues freely.

The best groups are led by a professional facilitator. This precludes any personal agenda from subconsciously directing the group. It also leaves the members free to participate in (rather than lead) the meeting. Professional facilitators who lead these groups are experienced in business, the psychology of group dynamics, presentation skills, and one-to-one coaching. Their skills are needed to assure that the meetings do not become superficial. They are responsible for and experts at achieving deeper levels of communication.

The one-to-one coaching aspect is not available, or advisable, in non-facilitated groups. Its purpose is to uncover and resolve deeper issues, as well as to discover topics that would be better discussed within the group. When these issues are presented properly, both the presenting member and the entire group grows from the discussion. The "coach" can also be utilized to facilitate issues within your own company. This is a distinct advantage and a great tool.

Issue presentation is a key activity in a good mastermind group. In the best cases, this is a three-step process. First, a member presents an issue to the group. Next is the discovery phase where members ask questions to clarify the issue. Finally, the members present solutions to the member who has presented the issue. If this is done right, everyone benefits.

Another primary benefit of the mastermind group is that it gives the entire membership the ability to get schooled in other businesses without having to work in them for a decade. Many "best practices" are discussed, and members walk away with information they can put to use immediately. Mastermind groups also hold one another accountable for achieving stated goals. It's very easy to let goals slide when no one is looking over your shoulder.

There are a number of business mastermind groups around the world. Perhaps the best known are the Young Presidents' Organization (YPO), Vistage (formally TEC), the Council of Growing Companies, and CEO Clubs. Each has its advantages. For example YPO is great for networking, and Vistage offers well-trained facilitators. The Council is comprised of very high growth companies, and CEO Clubs provides great speakers. You may have an idea to form your own group to assure that you get exactly what it is you want, but be careful that you are not reinventing the wheel. Choosing the right mastermind group does require some research.

I have been involved in mastermind groups for more than two decades, and they have been instrumental in my success as a businessman and a human being. If it's something you've thought about, I challenge you to take the risk of looking further. I promise you it will be well worth the investment of your time and money.

The Knowledge Lunch

The mark of a well-educated person is not necessarily in knowing all the answers, but in knowing where to find them.
—Douglas Everett

Would you like an idea that costs very little, but yields high returns? Of course you would. This technique will help you to make your company's lunch hour a training session for your team and add profit to the bottom line. The technique is called the Knowledge Lunch. This simple yet elegant practice helps your team members grow both personally and professionally. In addition, your company will profit from more educated and communicative team. Here's how it works.

Have each of your team members pick an industry or business publication that is valuable to your company and that they like; then subscribe to it for them. Pick a day of the week when the team agrees not to have out-of-the-office lunch appointments. (Wednesday seems to work for many organizations.) Have everyone select an article that they think will benefit the company and their fellow workers, or that they simply find interesting. Have them make copies of the article for each attendee (limit the group to 12). Then, as they are enjoying the lunchtime pizza (that you provide) they share a three- to five-minute summary of the article with the team.

Your staff will be keeping up with industry trends, learning new techniques, and educating each other. Your company will benefit from more knowledgeable workers and a tighter team. All for the price of pizza! There are also a couple of creative twists you can use for additional benefits.

There are many outside service companies (financial planners, industry sales reps, and so on) who would love to address an audience of potential clients. Think about bringing in a stockbroker to help educate your people in finances. This is important because when your team understands money well, they tend to treat company money/expenses with more respect. They will also benefit from continued lessons in dealing with their own finances. Companies that develop new products for your industry will also be very willing to address your team. For providers, it's an opportunity to display and promote their product. For your company, it's a way to keep workers educated about the latest advances in your industry. Best of all, the companies that provide this information will also buy lunch! Once a month, bring in an outside educator or vendor. It will add variety and new energy to your Knowledge Lunch.

During difficult economic times, one of the first things that most companies cut is training—even though it should be the last. This is a tried-and-true technique used by hundreds of businesses (during good and bad times) to save thousands of dollars and to continue educating their staff. Think about doing this at all levels within your company, and don't leave yourself out of the process. As a leader, knowing more about your industry may be the best advantage you have.

10 Reasons to Not Criticize an Ex-Mentor

Criticism is the disapproval of people, not for having faults,
but for having faults different from your own.
—Anonymous

Talking negatively about an ex-mentor or company can actually do damage in places where you might not expect it to. Here are 10 reasons to avoid being critical of a past employer.

1. Your current mentors and/or managers will automatically think that this is how you would talk about them if you change jobs, in or out of the company. Basically, it's just bad form, and you'll never look cool doing it.

2. Being the bigger person is so much better for your emotional well-being than being the opposite. It's helpful to accept that whomever you were working for brought something good into your life.

3. What goes around comes around. Call it karma if you like, but most of us have seen how this works, so why tempt fate? Keep the negativity to yourself, and trust that things will balance themselves out.

4. If you have any business dealings with your past mentors, it's going to make things very difficult if they think you've been bad-mouthing them. You never know where you'll end up. How many people do you know who are once again working for companies or with people who once let them go?

5. Everyone eventually tires of the same old song. Your co-workers or business associates may be too kind to tell you, so ask them if your behavior is over the top. Negative people aren't fun to do business with either, so maintain an appropriate attitude around clients and teammates.

6. Dwelling on the past is unhealthy emotionally. If you can't stop the thoughts in your head or get past the feelings on your own, it's usually a sign that you have some unfinished business.

7. Holding on to anger and pain is also physically unhealthy. Check yourself out and make sure you're not neglecting your body and hurting yourself. If you find that thoughts of your past co-workers or managers make you tighten your muscles, spend some time exercising and get a massage.

8. Feeling angry is a waste of time. If you're like the rest of us, you have far too many other, more positive things to put your time and energy into. Focus on your next goal or most recent accomplishments.

9. If you need to vent, do it with a professional. Maybe your current employer has an EAP (employee assistance plan) that offers some free therapy. This might be a good way to use that benefit. Just venting to your teammates can make them want to distance you.

10. The truth is that working with them wasn't all bad. Remember that you chose to work with your former mentor for a reason and that you probably learned a thing or two. In addition, just in terms of mental well-being, you deserve to keep your memories as nice as possible.

See this as an opportunity to make your life a better place as you remove a reason to not feel good about yourself. Remember that, every time you send out negative thoughts, you are also feeling them.

Leadership Skills

Being an emotionally in-tune leader is what Step 6 is all about. If you are unable to encourage effective emotions or cannot find the greatness within you, it will be difficult for you to motivate your team or yourself. Successful managers know the importance of pointing out what team members do right and realize that business issues start from the top down. Hiring well and knowing how to delegate and evaluate will give you the tools you need to take your company and your career to the next level.

Encouraging Effective Emotions at Work

When I repress my emotion my stomach keeps score.
—John Enoch Powell

Encouraging healthy emotions in the workplace is not only good for your team's interaction, from the board room to the assembly line—it is also good for your bottom line. Once your team members are able to really talk with each other, the blocks to risk taking, overcoming barriers and letting go of egos diminish. Here are 10 ways to encourage effective emotion in your company:

1. Resonate with your team and company. Once you are in tune with your job and your coworkers, it doesn't seem like work. Creating new ideas, working together in a positive manner, and feeling good about each other and what you are doing sounds more like satisfaction than work.

2. Problems start when team members stop talking. Without good communication, you might as well just hang the "closed" sign on the front door because eventually that's where you'll end up. If your staff and leaders can't talk about what they feel and need, not much will get accomplished.

3.   Give them someone to talk to. Have an open-door policy (either in your office or someone in HR) for team members to talk about issues that are bothering them. Fifteen minutes of being heard can change a person from a grumbling, non-productive, time-waster to a star producer for your company.

4.   Enforce the basic rules of effective communication. This is not rocket science; there are many chapters in this book that will help you get this started. I also suggest a refresher course every six months or so. We have to be reminded and encouraged to talk about our work-related problems in ways that are going to help solve them, not create new ones.

5.   Highly functional groups tend to be more relaxed. This goes much deeper than casual Fridays; it's about being emotionally relaxed. Let your people create their own work style (as long as it's not inappropriate). Implementers will gather with Innovators, tie-wearers will hang with the T-shirt crowd, and you will get a diverse mix of talent who will be more likely to speak up and share their ideas. It will make your people more involved, inspired, and productive. Give it a try at your next brainstorming session.

6.   Make sure your team's hearts and minds come to the office with them. Having bodies show up every day doesn't work if their passion isn't included. If people aren't emotionally invested in their job, or the people they work with, they won't do as good a job. For most individuals, work is about much more than money. They have to have an emotional attachment and get a little joy from the experience. Help them feel wanted and needed.

7.   Failures and missteps are a part of the success process. Hey, even Michael Jordan threw a few air-balls, and Babe Ruth also held the strike-out record. If you blew it, be honest and let your team know that you aren't perfect (this week). It will make you and your management team more human, and your staff will be more understanding. In addition, this behavior will help you eliminate the "us versus them" syndrome.

8. Create and idea-friendly environment. Many of your team members have had great ideas—or at least they used to. Somewhere along the line, if a person gets ignored or her ideas are squashed down, she won't be as likely to share them. When this happens, have a one-to-one conversation with the individual who may be holding back and let her know that you have appreciated her input in the past and would welcome it in the present.

9. Keep the emotional energy as upbeat as possible. When your company and/or team becomes comfortable with a negative atmosphere, it is a death knell. You must immediately inject some positive energy if you want to keep your business and team alive. Humor, being easygoing, and sharing how different it feels when everybody gets along and works together will help you keep the doors open and the paychecks coming.

10. Set the example: share your feelings. To help your team, start by sharing your emotional involvement with them and your company. Take the risk of actually honestly talking about your feelings and they will learn from your example. Just remember to set good boundaries as well and don't start talking about your breakups or unhappy childhood.

Utilizing emotions in an effective manner depends greatly on how you choose to integrate them into the consciousness of your company. This is a process, not an event. It is to be done slowly, over time. The benefits are boundless and will be felt sooner rather than later because everybody wants to talk about how they feel. Most are just waiting for someone they respect to listen.

54

Finding the Great Leader Within

Corporate leadership has lost the benefit of the doubt.
—Jeffery Imelt

What's happened to business leadership in the past few years? It's lost its credibility. Though yours may still be intact, what has the current climate done to your team's ability to take in and absorb your mission, vision, and values? Are you truly in alignment with your key people, and are they thinking appropriately for your company?

Think about the best boss you ever had. What is it about his or her leadership style that impresses you? Are you incorporating that style into your leadership techniques?

Now think about the worst boss you've ever had. What was it about his or her style that didn't work? Are you doing anything that resembles his or her mistakes?

These questions will help you understand your leadership style and what, if anything, needs to be changed. Finding out what kind of leader you are can be as simple as understanding the difference between being a uplifting leader or a penalizing leader.

Uplifting leaders inspire, help their team members stretch, and empower everyone they lead. Penalizing leaders take power away from their team members by burning out people and not giving energy to them.

How are you directing the thinking of your people? A true leader knows that performance starts with the thinking process. By teaching and motivating your team to think about what is best for the company and for the team members, you will help them develop a culture of cohesive workers.

What are you doing to create superior relationships with your direct reports and team members? What are they doing (or learning) to help inspire their teams? To make stars in your organization, you have to find ways to create relationships with your team that make them want to perform at a higher level.

The difference between average and star is the ability to blend all of your talents with the job at hand. People will rise to the occasion if they feel (yes, feel) they are doing the right thing, with the right people, for the right reason.

It is the leader's job to see what his or her team members need to create that blend and direct them to the proper individuals and resources to make it happen. The problem is that some leaders don't want to invest their time, energy, and money in their team members. They are unwilling to see that most growth actually comes from making mistakes. Leaders need to learn that their investment in their team members starts with allowing them to make mistakes—as long as those mistakes are admitted to and appropriately corrected.

The best way to initiate this practice is to not take away their problems. Don't give them the answers. Ask the necessary questions to make the team member think about and if necessary research what is needed to find the right answers. This is leadership in its purest form.

Allow your people to connect with you and they will mirror your leadership style. Simply by being in your presence and feeling how you do what you do, team members will take on the necessary abilities to get the job done in a very similar way that you would. To teach them, allow them to shadow you for a day every once in a while (monthly works best). Have a rising star follow you around and just observe. It will create a connection, give him new skills, and build his confidence.

Leading from within, and encouraging your team to grow and develop using the techniques outlined here will give your company the edge you need to thrive in the current climate. In addition, your attitude and the attitude of your team will also improve, and that alone will make your life and your business a much more productive (and pleasant) place to be.

The Leader Evangelist

Outstanding leaders appeal to the hearts of their followers—not their minds.

—Anonymous

Today's leader has to be an evangelist—no less of an evangelist than Billy Graham. If you watch the on-stage antics of Microsoft CEO Steve Balmer, you know he's proselytizing. He jumps around like Mick Jagger at a Rolling Stones concert and builds so much energy in the crowd that even die-hard Microsoft bashers become believers. His charisma is partly responsible for the company's success. Have you delivered that kind of energy to your teams, investors, and clients? If not, here are some ideas that can help you.

Just like John Lennon, who huddled the Beatles together before and after every gig to chant "Where are we going? To the top. Which top? The very top!" today's leader has to inspire their teams. Money will only rent people's time; they have to give you their hearts. This will only happen when they have faith in their leader and their company's vision.

Sometimes this takes as much explanation as inspiration. If your teams don't fully understand your vision and fully comprehend their place in it, they can't fully put their hearts there. Ask yourself, *Have I fully explained the vision for this company? Do my people "get it?" What can I do or say to help them understand, absorb and live the vision?* Put the vision in writing and make sure everyone sees it every day. Restate the vision at every meeting and keep it in your team's face. The more they see it and hear it, the more they will absorb it. I also recommend that you use it as a screen saver on all company computers.

It is also important to explain that this is "the vision," not your vision. When Walt Disney was building Disney World in Florida, he gathered all the engineers around a table and stated that he wanted Sleeping Beauty's Castle to be placed in the center of the park, and he wanted it to be the first thing built. The engineers protested and explained that it would cost him millions because it was more efficient to build from the outside in rather than the inside out. Walt said he didn't care about the money. It was more important that everyone involved in the project had a vision so that they could share in "the dream" (not his dream). The rest, as they say, is history.

Yes, we are talking about emotion, the most underutilized business tool at our command. Understanding how to utilize positive emotion is a leader's most powerful tool. If people feel positive about their company's vision they will exceed their own (and your) expectations. Positive feelings about their company inspire them to go the extra mile, stay the extra hour, and make the extra phone calls. Everyone needs to feel good about who they work for. It makes them proud to be a part of something that is bigger than they are. As long as they respect what they are doing and like their company, you will get more from them.

You have to be brutally honest with yourself and examine how you are utilizing the emotional power of your team. If you are being a hard-ass and just cracking the whip, you may be engaged in self-flagellation. In other words, you are only hurting yourself. Look, you don't have to like everyone that works for you; you're not renting friends. What you do have to do is get them to like you, and love their company. They have to feel good about what they are doing; it compels people to move ahead instead of treading water. Don't mistake being a leader with being a military commander. You need your people to create and implement, not seek and destroy.

The Non-Secret of
Successful Management

*A good leader takes a little more than his share of the blame,
a little less than his share of the credit.*
—Arnold H. Glasgow

What does it take to become a successful manager? The answer is simple. Start at the top, by encouraging and displaying total management commitment. Creating a best practices management program is a strategic process that requires an emotional focus. Posters, slogans, and seminars won't make it happen. How many companies do you know that talk about excellent management, but their skills (and bottom line) don't match up to their words? Without a true commitment to your team and your vision, an individual or team, regardless of education, training, and experience, can never hope to achieve excellence in management skills.

Valuable lessons

Treat team members as you do your boss. Some managers, when they are promoted, let their insecurity get the best of them and begin to lead by intimidation. Excellent managers create a team where staff members feel valued and equal. The payoff is more energy, more respect, and a greater desire to work together, not to mention the bottom-line results. Lesson: Eliminate the word *employee*. Use *staff* or *team member*, and treat them as such.

Don't worry about who's right. Worry about what's right. The first step in problem solving is to find out what the real problem is. Great managers ask themselves if they are part of the problem. Facing the issue and gaining awareness are the next two steps. When blame is cast, learn to look at the blamers. What are they pretending not to know? Lesson: Don't believe the blamers. Get the whole story before making a decision.

Lead by example; it's more valuable than advice

If the leaders are apathetic or condescending, that attitude will flow through the entire company. The results are poor performance and ultimately a decrease in profits. Leaders need to roll up their sleeves and join forces with the team. For example, consider the example set by Herb Kellerhern of Southwest Airlines, who is known for loading luggage on Thanksgiving, or that of Andy Grove of Intel, whose office was a cubicle like the rest of the staff. Those teams rise to the occasion. Lesson: Always act as you think these (or your) chairman would act—no matter what the situation is.

The dynamics of support: building an effective team

In today's marketplace it's very rare to find any success story that doesn't involve partnership or teamwork. Even on the rare occasion of a one-person operation climbing to the top, you'll usually find that individual having some sort of strong support, be it financial, emotional or spiritual. The business economy is more complex and global in nature now. The simple truth is: we need each other. The deeper truth is we need to deal with each other on a regular basis so we best learn how to do it right. There are many common albeit unnecessary mistakes made in a few basic areas that, if dealt with or approached from a different and more creative angle, could heal most problems in today's workplace. The dynamics that go on inside most companies are incredible. They include everything ranging from highly productive yet excessively angry, backbiting coworkers (a poisonous environment) to the other end of the scale: a too-laid-back, unorganized workplace, where deadlines are missed because nobody wants to "be the bad guy." Both scenarios are losing propositions because resentment usually takes over and decays the infrastructure. Coaches, mentors, and connected team members are a necessity to create and sustain a winning company.

Reward and recognition

Thank you. These are the two most important words in the English language. Yet many people are absolutely oblivious to thanking others for the magnificent jobs they do day in and day out. It is simply astounding. What's even more astonishing is that most people not only don't recognize others, but they don't recognize themselves and the contributions they make to their companies.

Once the commitment is made, there are ways to raise the bar of management excellence. For example, the number-one mistake is not complimenting employees often. Leaders (managers, executive staff, CEOs and owners) are celebrities to their staffs. A pat on the back can uplift and motivate your team to reach higher than ever. It is a simple task, but many managers hold back praise. They believe that being too "nice" will give team members permission to slack off. Quite the opposite is true. Studies at UCLA's Anderson School of Management show that a little praise and recognition from an executive will create more motivation than anything else, including money. Lesson: Publicly reward team members who have good ideas or perform beyond expectations

Recognition also keeps communication open, which again is your lifeline to your staff. Silence can be easily misinterpreted. How many cases have resulted in an upper level management executive losing his or her right-hand man simply because of the lack of communication? Think about it. If a valued staff member never hears word one, good nor bad, about the quality of his or her work, the assumption is likely to that the individual is not pleasing his or her boss and that his or her work is unsatisfactory. What's likely to happen is that the individual will become frustrated and find another position, choose to participate but just phone it in, or retire or quit.

That's why it's important to keep communication alive and vibrant with your staff. Attack problems when they arise. Trust your intuition. If you "feel" like there is a 800-pound gorilla in the room no one is talking about, talk about it. Open the lines of communication, and stay in touch with your staff's needs and desires. Foster an atmosphere of cooperation, and give credit where credit is due. In return, you will have a team that will go the extra hundred miles for you, and the returns will be tenfold.

Remember: When you are passionate about their involvement and contributions, there will be no limit to the success you can achieve.

57

Catch 'em Doing Something Right

Leadership is action, not position.
—Donald H. Mcgannon

If your team is interacting negatively with each other, it could be a fatal flaw in your company. Don't call in the CSI team just yet. How about detecting the great things your team members do? For some, pointing out what isn't working is much easier than rewarding someone for a great effort, but at what cost?

Sit down with your team and discuss how you relate, and, if you agree that there needs to be a change, you are halfway to a solution. If team members and leaders are continually nit-picking, and point fingers at one another, you have a problem that needs to be corrected in the near term. To start you must acknowledge its existence and agree that everyone involved wants these negative actions to change.

The next step to create some emotional balance in your company culture is to catch your team members doing something right and tell them when you see it. Remember that recognition from the company leader has been proven to be the number-one motivator

213

of staff members. The tangible proof that this technique works will show up in your bottom line.

You need to set policy to eliminate negative emotional behaviors if you want to survive the downturn. Plain and simple. All changes have to start at the top and, if you're guilty of being overbearing, let the changes begin with you. If it's your team leaders, have a serious sit down and train them to make necessary changes.

Joe Phelps, CEO of the Phelps Group, is a great example of how this process works. Joe strongly encourages his team members to "Be Kind. Be Clear. Be Constructive. Be Candid." These words of wisdom have helped his company grow to one of the top independent marketing communications companies in Los Angeles.

Taking responsibility for discord is another very powerful way of lifting your company to the next level. If people in a conflict realize that they are each completely responsible for the problems, it actually eliminates the issue because it gives you and your staff the ability to change how you work together. From downturns to riots, this technique has been used by successful companies and city governments to iron out the most difficult problems.

For everyone to experience the productivity that comes with cohesion, keep checking in on how well everyone is working together. Offer team members an opportunity to discuss their experiences, both good and bad, so you can continually refine the process.

Current circumstances can apply pressure that will bring out the worst in people, and sometimes you just have to get the frustration out of your system. Having some after-hours fun can help team members release a lot of pent-up tension.

Trusting that a kind word or direction can make or break a company may be hard for some old-school leaders to digest. The truth is that we have to change the way we do business or we will never succeed again.

58

The Fish Stinks
From the Head Down

*Ethics must begin at the top of an organization. It is a
leadership issue and the chief executive must set the example.*
—Edward Hennessy

This old saying simply means that the leader is responsible for
everything and anything in their company. That means everything
that goes right, and anything that goes wrong. Good leadership and
management are the most important functions of any business.
Simply put, bad leadership equals bad business.

The 4 components of a business

To better understand this vital concept, let's look at the four
components of any business:

1. Management, which lives in the present.
2. Marketing, which lives in the future.
3. Finance, which lives in the past.
4. Operations, which always costs you money.

When entropy (the tendency of a system to run down) begins to happen, an imbalance that may not be obvious to the leader of a company is beginning to occur. When the leader is unaware of trouble that is brewing in any of the four components, the "fish begins to stink."

If the object of business is to make money, and when you make bad decisions in any of the above components, it will cost you. You need to be aware of, and have balance between, the four components. That means that you need to "cast a wide net" so that you are conscious of everything and everyone around you. Your mindfulness of your business needs to be as adept as the fisherman looking for the biggest catch. If you do not "cast your net" in the right place, you may miss an opportunity, or, worse, be eaten by your competition.

Hire slower, fire faster

One of the biggest mistakes leaders make is to hire too fast and fire too slow. Make this process more productive and less painful by letting your managers or teams be actively involved in the hiring. Successful business leaders know that, when staffing, people tend to hire in their own mode—like attracts like (because it makes us more comfortable). Also remember that you lead by what you tolerate, so, if you or your managers tolerate insubordination, you will hire insubordinate people. Leaders need to find ways to help their teams become aware of their tolerance levels and avoid hiring in their own mode.

Begin by creating a profile of the job and the right person for it. To make the hiring procedure much easier, try using an objective behavioral assessment tool. These tests will run you anywhere from $200 to $500 each. There are dozens you can take for free online including one I've created. The Goldsmith Innovation/Implementation Index (g3i) can be found on my Website. Remind your managers and yourself to take the time and do the research necessary before bringing anyone into a position of responsibility, and, once hired, invest in training them properly for the job.

In the long run, a few dollars spent in proper training will not only save you, but make you much, much more. Training is not an HR issue, it's like giving your children to a neighbor and saying "raise them as I would." Look at how you learned what you know, and create ways to help your teams learn what they need to know. Give them the tools to do the best job possible. A well-trained team member will improve your efficiency, company morale, and bottom line.

Is your fish fresh?

Now that you have been reminded that "the fish stinks from the head down," you will be more vigilant about your role as the leader. Remembering that management is the most important component of your business, and that the buck stops with you, will give you greater ability to create balanced teams (with both Innovators and Implementers), to hire slower, to train better, and to see your part in any problems. These tools will help you to keep "your fish" (your business) fresh.

Dr. G's Questions for Effective Hiring

Leaders create an environment in which everyone has the opportunity to do work which matches his potential capability.
—Elliott Jaques

Hiring is an emotional process for everyone involved. Understanding a prospect's emotional drives (as well as the interviewer's) is key to finding and keeping the right people. Certain interview questions can illicit responses that will tell you how a person is feeling about himself, your company, if he is a team player, and how he will react under stress.

The questions I like to ask may seem a bit cryptic, or even touchy-feely. The object here is to require the prospect not just to think, but to feel. This way, you can understand what truly drives them. Whatever their emotional drivers may be, they will become obvious by how they answer the questions.

Here is a list of questions that I think tell the whole truth about how someone will participate in your work environment.

These first four questions will tell you if the prospect is a team player:

219

- Do you prefer to be evaluated as part of a work team or on your own accomplishments?
- Have you ever played team sports or been a member/ leader of an organization? (Boy/Girl Scouts, Rotary, etc.)
- Do you prefer to take or give direction?
- Which is more comfortable for you?

This next set of questions will define whether the person wants to grow professionally:

- What did you learn from your co-workers at your last place of employment?
- What are you willing to commit to, to make this company and yourself better?
- Do you see yourself as an Innovator or an Implementer?
- Are you willing to implement or innovate if necessary?

The following questions will help you see where this person's talents can best be used:

- Describe your dream position.
- If you were away from the office and could only make one phone call a day, what questions would you ask?
- What issues at any of your former jobs kept you up at night?
- Who was the best mentor you have had in business and what made him or her the best?

These questions tell you more than just what a person thinks, they tell you *how* the person thinks. They not only give you information about what a person is capable of, they tell you how the person is going to feel about the job and the people he or she works with. If someone feels negative or uncomfortable about your company or the people in it, you will not get the performance you need to build a business winning team.

Emotions are our driving force, and they cannot be pushed aside. Control of emotions is an illusion because a person's true feelings will always be projected in one fashion or another. Nothing unsaid ever goes unnoticed, so remain aware of how your prospect reacts to these deeper questions. Understanding someone's emotional reactions to his or her job will help you prevent hiring someone who will not just under perform, but who is capable of undermining your business.

Do You Run Your Business or Does It Run You?

It is a terrible thing to look over your shoulder when
you are trying to lead—and find no one there.
—Franklin D. Roosevelt

Ask yourself if you are working "in" rather than "on" your business? For example, are you spending too much time dealing with the day-to-day aspects of running your company? That time should be spent creating business development or long-term business goals. If this is the case, there may be several obstacles that are keeping you from achieving your goals.

Are you having cash-flow issues that are keeping you from thinking about growth or hiring people to do the management tasks? Are your management skills up to par, do you have the insights necessary to see the big picture, or are you feeling safer just dealing with what's in front of you? These are two situations that can keep you from taking the steps necessary to grow your company.

If you are in a high-risk business, the stress could be keeping you from a strategic focus. This may require more than stress-management; you may need to bring in some outside money or talent to help you get things under control. There may also be a lack of systems and infrastructure, which again require bringing in some additional help to get the proper systems integrated into your company.

Additional obstacles may also be that you have nothing else to do, in which case you need to find a niche where you can do what you do best. Lastly, being in a business where you sell your time (independent contractor/consultant/professional) can prevent you from seeing the growth potential or new products and services that can increase your bottom line.

A lack of trust in your people could also be stealing your time. If you feel you are the only one who can do it right and withhold delegation, there's going to be too much on your plate, and you're paying for services that you're not using. You need to have a balanced level of trust with every member of your team. That level of trust dictates how much responsibility you can really hand off. It is within your power to expand that level; it is also within your power to keep it the same.

If you want more freedom in your business, you must expand your level of trust. If you're going to grow a functional organization, one that grows exponentially, you have to hand off some of the power. Ask yourself: Since you started in business, how much power have you given up? How have you given it up? Have you done it in a way that doesn't keep you up at night and doesn't cause you to jump back in at the first sign of trouble? Remember: When you give someone responsibility, you also have to give them authority.

There's a fine line between handing off the power and the team member's ability to handle the power. Ask yourself: what does your team member want in exchange to own the power? It's a good idea to ask the team member as well. Finding innovative ways to reward team members for taking on additional tasks is key here. At Magellan's, a catalogue and Internet travel supplies company located in Santa Barbara, CEO John McManus has a strong team that he can leave in charge when he does what he loves best, which is travel. One of his tactics is to reward team members for finding new hires that are capable and trustworthy. He pays a bounty of a few hundred dollars, as well as giving his team the responsibilities they desire in addition to those he requires.

Find a way of doing business that keeps good people on board and draws the right people in. What you focus on expands—what we do more of, we become more aware of. If you don't have a board of advisors or mastermind group to help you, that's your starting point. Let them help you create a realistic vision, and from that you will see the paths of possibility. Your board or group, and your team need to be empowered to hold each other accountable. With this kind of foundation, you can build anything.

The Awesome Power of the Company Evaluation

The only things that evolve by themselves in an organization are disorder, friction, and mal-performance.
—Peter Drucker

To manage the future growth of your company and your people, it's important to have a benchmark of where you are today. Sounds obvious, but how many CEOs have ever done a company evaluation to find out what everyone in the company thinks about how the organization is running/doing? This process is one of the most valuable tools for companies today. What executives can learn from the people in your organization, some of which you may never see, is astounding. One good idea from someone on the firing line can generate millions. Everyone from the janitor, to customer service professionals to line managers sees things CEOs don't, and they all have ideas they think will work. What we have to realize as leaders is their ideas are as valuable to us as the feedback and direction we get from our most trusted advisors.

This evaluation process makes team members feel top management cares about what they think. If people feel that their ideas are valued, they will perform better and will more readily step outside their boxes to tackle your company's current challenges. The sense of empowerment that team members get when they feel that their opinions are valued can put them on a productive high for weeks. This will give them more motivation and energy than a closet full of Tony Robbins books. No only will your team feel you care about them and their ideas, but your company will get a burst of creativity and intense activity, too.

Leaders always want to know how to get their team members to make a greater commitment or how to get them to take ownership of their teams and assignments. Doing a company evaluation will not only reinforce commitment and allow them to feel ownership, but it will assist top management in creating team-building and progressive thinking as a company culture

Use simple, generic questions designed to lead to insight and introspection. Make sure they encourage employees to think of themselves in relation to their jobs, and their responses help top management understand how well it communicates with its people. This is a merely a starting point. Some organizations may want to eliminate some of their first choices and create others that are more company-specific, but keep the number of questions asked to no more than 12 in all. If you don't the exercise may seem like a homework assignment and could end up in a circular file somewhere.

Make sure team members have the option of anonymity. Some people will fear reprisal if they "tell it like it is." Offer a reward to the team members whose ideas you use. This will encourage them to identify themselves. For small ideas, the rewards should not be large. Consider movie tickets or company logo wear (polo shirts, hats, and so forth). For ideas that make you money, trips, vacation time or bonuses are appropriate. This approach is just good common sense. If a team member creates prosperity for a company, then that person should be taken care of. Look at it this way: if your brother-in-law introduced you to someone who became a large client, you'd probably buy him a set of golf clubs—right? Rewarding your people sends a message that you care and that they can make their lives better by taking a risk and implementing their ideas.

Once a company decides to implement an evaluation program, remember that participants will want to know what is happening with the evaluations. A word to the wise: Be prepared to dive into these and get results back to your team within two weeks. Consider planning an event to announce the results, and publicly reward those ideas the company is going to use.

Use an evaluation at least once a year. What the company will learn can increase the bottom line and pay off greatly in other areas such as the people side of the business. The results that follow will be enlightening, humbling, and downright awesome.

Here are some sample questions. It is best to ask for suggestions as well as constructive criticism from those who do the evaluation.

Emotional Fitness
Company Evaluation Questions

- What does the company need to do to continue to succeed/survive?
- What can I do to help?
- What talents do I have that I am not using on this job?
- How can this company utilize my talents in a better way?
- What is the level of financial fear in the company (1 most fearful—10 most safe)?
- What is my level of financial fear (1 most fearful—10 most safe)?
- What can be done to make everyone feel safer in this environment?
- What can I do to make the company feel safer?
- What is it that we are best at?
- What is it that I am best at?
- What can be done to make the staff a stronger team?
- What can I contribute to make the staff a stronger team?
- What can the leaders do more of to inspire us to do our best?
- What can I do to inspire the leaders to do their best?

20 Leadership Tools You Can Use

Great leaders have one thing in common—passion!
—Barton Goldsmith

These are my top 20 best practices that I have seen used by the most successful leaders. Some of these are already in your toolkit, others you may have forgotten. Keep this list handy as a reminder of time tested solutions that will make you and your team shine.

1. Use the power of the pen. Recognition is the number-one motivator. A simple thank-you note is more important than money to most people. Break out the fancy pen you got for your birthday and say thanks to the people who helped to get you there.

2. Understand the importance of emotions. Feelings are a part of daily life and daily business. When people get hurt feelings they become poor performers, so make sure you deal with these issues sooner rather than later.

3. Great leaders have one thing in common: passion! If you're not turned on about what you're doing, your team won't be either, so show them that you're excited and watch them get fired up.

4. Communication is the most important thing in any business relationship. If you don't use effective business communication skills you're leaving money on the table and not getting the most out of your people. Don't be afraid to take a brush-up course and listen to hints from those who are in the positions you want. Chances are they got there because they're great communicators.

5. Do a company evaluation at least once a year. Ask your team members to respond in writing to important questions like "What do we need to change?" and "What do we need to keep doing more of?" This is your most powerful tool for a 50,000-foot view of your business.

6. Create a company mentoring program. Every person in and entering your company should have a mentor. A mentor's job is to help a new or junior staff member feel welcomed as well as to answer any questions. Having a mentor builds confidence and creates motivation to go above and beyond.

7. Make sure your teams are balanced with both Innovators and Implementers. If everyone on a team is an Innovator, nothing will get done. Similarly, a team of only Implementers will create nothing new. To make sure you have a balanced team, utilize the free test (called the g3i) on the Website *www.BartonGoldsmith.com*.

8. Remember that customer service rocks. The two most profitable customer service tips I have used are a full return/ refund policy, which eliminates risk on the part of your client and encourages them to "step up to the plate"; and never saying "no" to clients. This policy creates the opportunity for you and your client to find other ways to do business together, rather than you telling them you can't or don't provide a particular service or product.

9. Achieve goals by getting team member buy-in. If your people have input into your goals they will put more energy into helping you achieve them. Ask them what they think and you'll get their dedication in return.

10. Implement a Knowledge Lunch. Keep your team up to date by having a lunch meeting once a week where you discuss your business. You can even bring in vendors and financial advisors (who will buy the pizza) to help keep your team connected and current.

11. Deal appropriately with fear in the workplace. When team members are in fear for their livelihood (and in these times perhaps fear of their lives), they do not perform at their highest level. Providing a forum to safely talk about these fears will go a long way toward helping achieve superior performance.

12. Don't just be a manager; be an evangelist. You need to believe in what you and your company are doing and to share the power of that belief with your team members. A good leader can't become great if he or she doesn't inspire faith in the company.

13. Pursue failure. Failure is not an ending it is a stepping stone to the right answer. Stop beating yourself up for mistakes and see them as an opportunity to begin again with additional information, knowledge, and experience.

14. Remember that the fish stinks from the head down. That means everything that you are responsible for everything that goes right, and anything that goes wrong. Remembering that leadership is the most important component of your business and that the buck stops with you will help you keep your "fish" fresh.

15. Having fun increases productivity and profit. In companies where people have fun, the productivity and the profit are higher. The American Psychological Association has published surveys about this, and it's a fact. Take the example of Southwest Airlines: do you know that "a sense of humor" is on their job application?!

16. Beware of invalidation. The number one motivation killer is making a team member feel "less than." If you mistakenly say the wrong thing to someone, apologize immediately. You'll look like a responsible leader rather than an insensitive bully.

17. Learn to maintain your composure under pressure. Thomas Jefferson said, "Nothing gives one person so much advantage over another as to remain cool and unruffled under all circumstances."

18. Join a mastermind group. To keep your skills sharp and get answers to difficult questions get into a group of non-competing peers. The greatest minds in business have used mastermind groups to help them excel in their chosen fields.

19. Learn to ask powerful questions. The right question at the right time can eliminate major problems or help a team member find the best answer available.

20. Learn to deal with difficult people. There are specific techniques to deal with different types of people. Learn how to tell avoidance from arrogance and denial from insecurity.

These tried-and-true tips will help guide you to make the right decisions at the right times, for the right reasons. Leadership is an art form, and the best of the best use many of these proven techniques.

Index

About the Author

Named by the national press as one of the country's top experts, award-winning psychotherapist, syndicated columnist, and radio host, Barton Goldsmith, PhD, is an internationally recognized business consultant, author, and speaker. He has appeared on CNN, *Good Morning America*, *Fox & Friends*, *CBS News*, *NBC News*, *Beauty and the Geek*, and *The Greg Behrendt Show*. In addition, numerous radio shows and national magazines have interviewed him. Most recently, Dr. Goldsmith served as the national spokesperson for the Mars Candy My M&M's Treasured Moments Challenge.

His popular monthly business column has appeared in more than 300 publications, including *Entrepreneur*, *The Atlanta Journal Constitution*, *The Los Angeles Business Journal*, *Office Solutions*, *Successful Meetings*, and *Brilliant Results*. Since 2002, his weekly column, Emotional Fitness, which is syndicated by Scripps-Howard News Service, has run in the *Chicago Sun-Times*, the *Ventura County Star*, the *Orange County Register*, the *Detroit News*, the *Cincinnati Post*, the *San Diego Union-Tribune*, and more than 200 other newspapers, giving him a readership in the millions. His column ranks in the top third of everything the News Service sends out.

In addition, Dr. Goldsmith hosts a weekly radio show on the most award-winning station in Southern California, KCLU/NPR, with 80,000 listeners in Los Angeles, Ventura, and Santa Barbara, where he discusses business and personal issues with a strong fan base.

Dr. Goldsmith is also an accomplished and engaging speaker and has delivered numerous presentations to businesses and associations worldwide. He was a Chairman for The Executive Committee (TEC) and a forum leader and resource speaker for the Young Presidents Association (YPO). He also sits on several boards including Ribbon of Hope and advises successful companies throughout the United States.

Dr. Goldsmith was a National Merit Scholar and a professor at Ryokan College. He received recognition from the City of Los Angeles for his work with survivors of the 1994 earthquake. Dr. Goldsmith is the 2007 winner of the Clark Vincent Award and the 2006 Peter Markin Merit Award for his humanitarian efforts. He was also named as the 2006 recipient of the Joseph A. Giannantoino Award in recognition of his contributions as an Outstanding Educator.

"Dr. G" began working in the field of psychology and business when his career in professional basketball was cut short because he only grew to 5 foot 6 inches tall.